Contents

D1473569

Editorial

Much development thought has dismissed religion, its rituals and its customs, as at best irrelevant and at worst a barrier to economic, social, and political 'progress'. This collection of articles – by writers who live both within, and outside, various religious traditions – explores these views. Why have considerations of faith and spirituality been left on the margin of development research, practice, and policy, not only by 'mainstream' development, but by many gender and development workers? This marginalisation of a critical area of human activity has had, and continues to have, a dramatic negative impact on economic, social, and political development, and the attainment of equality for women.

Moving beyond this, contributors to this collection also analyse the complex relationship between culture, religion, and feminism, and how this is played out in gender and development work in countries of the South. They aim to assess how both organised religions, and personal spiritual convictions can shape, challenge, and potentially transform gender relations.

Religious faith and its institutions

As Bridget Walker states in her article, religion can have a contradictory status in women's lives. The close relationship between core religious beliefs, and religious institutions with their associated rituals and customs, means that the distinction between these is often overlooked. This blurring of terms has led to further confusion in much development literature, where the terms 'culture' and 'religion' are used almost interchangeably to describe any or all of these elements (Mukhopadhyay 1995). A key feminist strategy has been to highlight the distinction between the two, described by one writer as the difference between 'religion' and 'religiosity' (Carroll 1983).

Women's position within societies is regulated by religious institutions at the family and community levels. Custom and tradition, often justified on religious grounds, ensure women's conformity to conventional gender roles, which can be the source of powerlessness and pain. In particular, notions of fatalism which are integral to many religions, from Hinduism to Orthodox Christianity, can offer comfort to the powerless and an explanation for suffering, while at the same time constraining people from seeking change.

Religious 'fundamentalism' and the control of women

The connections between religion, culture, and the control of women are evident throughout the history of human development. Women's central role as wives, mothers, and transmitters of cultural and religious beliefs (Mukhopadhyay 1995) makes it important for their behaviour to be regulated, in particular their sexuality, since the paternity of their children is of prime concern to patriarchal societies. 'Most human religions, from tribal to world religions, have treated woman's body, in its gender-specific sexual functions, as impure or polluted and thus to be distanced from sacred spaces and rites dominated by males' (Radford Ruether 1990, 7). The need to control women's impure sexuality is linked to male physical and mental violence against them, ranging from the sexual violence inflicted on child and adult females at home and outside the home, to the policing of women's dress codes and 'modesty'.

Several articles in this issue, and many of the resources listed at the end of this collection, address the threat to women's human rights from religious extremists in the many politically unstable situations all over the world, who use the control of women as a symbol of social cohesion. Although often misleadingly associated solely with Islam, the emphasis on a return to 'fundamental' religious laws actually originates in American Protestant Christianity. 'Fundamentalists' are defined by one source as having 'a militant desire to defend religion against the onslaughts of modern, secular culture; their principal weapon is their insistence on the inerrancy of scripture' (Hawley and Proudfoot 1994, 3). Fundamentalism's basic concern is attaining political power through control of social structures, rather than an intrinsic interest in religious truth (ibid.). (For further analysis and information on strategies to eradicate the issue of violence against women, including violence inflicted in the name of religion or culture, see *Gender and Development* Vol. 6, No. 3, November 1998.)

Development, culture, and feminism

The same complex relationship between political and economic power, and the control of women through culture and religion, could be seen during colonialism, when Western Christianity was exported to the empires of European states. Attempts to 'domesticate' women in the colonies into nineteenth-century European ideals of wife- and motherhood accompanied the message of Christianity brought by the missionaries (Hansen 1992, referring to Africa).

In the post-colonial era, a growing number of development workers from former colonial powers have been anxious to avoid charges of cultural and religious imperialism. Accordingly, they have worked 'around' these issues, focusing on practical, technical, or material issues (Ver Beek, forthcoming). However, it is increasingly argued that for development agencies to ignore the religious beliefs of the people with whom they work, or to reject them out of hand as backward or 'against development', itself amounts to a continuation of cultural imperialism which is promoting secularism. All too frequently, the failure of development interventions is explained by 'blaming the traditionalism of an ill-defined, but convenient, idea of "culture"' (Crewe and Harrison 1999, 1).

Southern feminists working in development have been particularly keen to challenge the idea of culture as a separate, backward realm of life which outsiders may respect or denigrate, but in which they should not interfere (Longwe 1995, 47). Southern feminists have argued that such cultural relativity is patronising, and potentially allows women's rights to be marginalised. However, Southern feminists risk accusations of betraying their societies if they criticise the cultural and religious status of women (Mukhopadhyay 1995). In view of the complex interplay between race, religion, and gender, and in an atmosphere of accusations and counter-accusations of racism and sexism, you need courage to take action. In her article, Fatima L Adamu discusses how the tensions between gender and race turn into a 'double-edged sword' for Muslim feminists working in Northern Nigeria. As Adamu states, they must not only challenge the prejudices of men from their own communities regarding their view of 'gender' as a Western imposition, but also circumvent the corresponding prejudice of foreign donors against Islam. Haleh Afshar has summed up this hostility as follows: 'just as in the West much of the discussion about Islam and Islamist women is conducted in terms of simplistic caricatures, so it is in the case of the perception of Western feminism by the establishment [in Iran]' (Afshar 1998, 33).

Such tensions are particularly evident in situations where culture is perceived to be under threat, for example in immigrant communities. In her article on Pakistani male violence in Bradford, UK, Marie Macey analyses how notions of racism, religion, culture, and feminism have paralysed institutional responses in this context to male violence against women both inside and outside the home.

In her article, Stacey Burlet traces how the Hindu religion has become linked to struggles for political power and notions of nationhood in India. Many NGOs and community-based organisations (CBOs) are currently upholding the ideal of secular development which the Indian state embraced at independence. They resist being drawn into the polarised political struggles around the idea of Hindus as one united nation, and emphasise that poverty cuts across religious differences. As Burlet states, NGOs and CBOs must achieve a difficult balancing act between acknowledging religious affiliation as an important aspect of personal identity, and privileging it above other aspects of economic and social differentiation. The Indian women's movement in particular is facing this challenge to its agenda.

Religion and transformation

Oppressive interpretations of religious texts promoted by male-dominated religious institutions can be challenged by alternative interpretations of religious writings, and, as Bridget Walker states in her article, these feminist theologies can be compared and linked to other liberation theologies which reclaim religion for the poor (Walker 1987). The core ideas of a religion, often expressed in the words of a deity or prophet, can inspire positive social, economic, and political change. Religious faith motivates the thoughts and actions of women and men throughout the world; most religious movements have their roots in transformatory visions, which focus on the 'inner ethical motivations of the person, rather than their external bodily state, and respect for all persons, regardless of gender or ethnicity' (Radford Ruether 1990, 14, on Christianity and modern reformist Judaism).

In line with this, Iman Hashim challenges Islam's reputation for being 'anti-woman', and supportive of a 'segregated social system where women are economically and politically marginalised' (Hashim, this issue, p.8). She, with other Muslim women and men, argues that women can fight for the attainment of political, social, and economic rights from within the framework of Islam. These arguments emphasise the importance of reclaiming the egalitarian spirit of many religious texts, to counter the current life-and-death threat presented to women in many contexts by religious extremists, often termed 'fundamentalists'. However, as Sadia Ahmed describes in her article on religious extremism in Somalia, this is only useful for the majority if women at the grassroots can gain access to these arguments. It is they whose bodies become battlegrounds for competing interpretations of religious texts, and they who require both basic education and knowledge of religious texts and arguments as weapons against fundamentalist interpretations of Islam.

From a Christian perspective, in her article on World Vision's approach to gender issues, development worker Linda Tripp continues the theme of countering sexism through reclaiming religious texts. World Vision uses the Gospels of the life of Christ to assert the equal humanity of women, and to promote their rights through development programmes. This has also included implementing a gender policy within World Vision itself. Tripp also discusses the advocacy work on spiritual values in development undertaken by World Vision, which was instrumental in persuading the Canadian International Development Agency (CIDA) to determine a formal position on the role of spirituality and religion in its work.

The myth of 'value-free' development

As gender analysis and other forms of social analysis have shown, no forms of change or 'development' (even those concerned with technical change) are value-free, and all of them have an impact on culture and power relations in society (Longwe 1995). Donors' reluctance to fund development initiatives with links to religious bodies often stems from a real concern for the potentially negative consequences for communities. However, as Fatima Adamu argues (p.60), this means that some community-based organisations in the South are obliged to struggle on their own. Others accept resources from donors who at best ignore, and at worst encourage them to reject, their commitment to religious belief. In effect this kind of development, presented as value-free, is actually preaching what Linda Tripp terms a 'doctrine of secularity' (p.66), which marginalises many human concerns. A conceptual separation of physical well-being from spiritual health is alien to many cultures and belief-systems, having its roots in Western notions of science and medicine (Joseph 1990).

In their article, Sharon Harper and Kathleen Clancy discuss how research for development could integrate spiritual values and religious beliefs, and argue that development researchers and workers should acknowledge that the true goal of human development involves more than material wealth, or even well-being; it is also about intangibles including personal fulfilment and happiness. In their discussion, Harper and Clancy draw on the preliminary findings of the Science, Research and Development (SRD) Project of the Canadian International Development Research Centre (IDRC). Building on the fact that some 'factors which influence people's world-view, such as gender, indigenous knowledge and social structure' have already been addressed in development, Harper and Clancy argue for 'being-oriented' research approaches for development, which draw on individual and shared ideas of spirituality.

Integrating religion into impact assessment

Recording, and learning from, cultural or religious change is essential if the impact of development interventions on various groups is to be assessed. There have been recent calls from UNRISD and UNESCO for the development of cultural indicators, including individual and social well-being (UNRISD, 1997, quoted by Baha'i Publishing Trust, 1998).

Catherine Dolan considers the changing patterns of religious worship and the growing use of witchcraft among women in Meru District, Kenya. Dolan links these directly to women's resentment of economic marginalisation and of the overwork they have suffered as a result of the introduction of export horticulture. Women use poison to injure and tranquillise their husbands as a strategy of resistance, and convert to 'born-again' Christianity to find the mental and emotional strength to withstand current pressures. Rather than dismissing these phenomena as unrelated to the economic changes that are taking place, or as proof of 'backwardness', Dolan argues that they indicate serious flaws in the development model used in Meru. The spiritual domain has become the principal forum in which struggles over land and labour are expressed; these struggles could not only undermine the economic objectives of export horticulture, but also lead to familial breakdown. Ultimately, they prove the poverty of vision in economic models of 'development', which merely aim to increase income rather than well-being. In turn, Rebecca Saul's comparative study of two communities in north-western Nepal demonstrates the dynamism of religious belief in response to economic and social change. She explores how Buddhist rituals are changing in significance and nature in response to the growing tourist trade. 'Development' based on tourism is having a profound impact on community life in one of the settlements, Saul argues; in contrast, the second community has chosen a different kind of development and kept their religious traditions.

Conclusion

Articles in this collection survey the impact of religion and spirituality on women's lives, on communities, and on development work. Writers argue that human development must rest on personal, and organisational, commitment to values beyond the individualism and materialism characteristic of world development to date. Research into gender and organisational change illustrates the importance of the link between the commitment of individual workers, and their success or failure in achieving certain goals (Porter et al. 1999). In line with this, there is an increasing awareness that all development workers who promote poverty alleviation with social justice must practise what they preach if they hope to extend their scope to influence global political and economic players: 'it is the link between values and actions that is crucial in generating legitimacy when arguing the case for change'(Edwards and Sen 1999, 11).

But what precisely is the relationship between personal commitment to social justice and religious or spiritual beliefs? While 'development, being concerned with the ordering of social life, is at root a moral issue, and moral systems have generally sprung from and been underwritten by spiritual sources' (ibid., 2), it is, surely, critically important to maintain a clear distinction between established religions and their institutions, personal spirituality, and the values of moral activism which underlie compassionate and equitable human development (Francis 1999).

Nevertheless, the current interest in spirituality is a welcome opportunity to consider links between individual faith, social institutions, and the shared ethics and values on which we base our communities. To date, it has been difficult to find a vocabulary to debate these issues in development organisations which do not have a religious foundation. Reasons for this difficulty include a legitimate fear of imposing ideologies on colleagues and partners in development, especially because of the negative effects of religious extremism on societies, and particularly women, across the world. 'The rising tide of religious bigotry across the world in recent decades is one of the reasons why space for serious discussion on the links between social and personal change has been so closed off' (Edwards and Sen 1999, 7). Perhaps now is the time for that discussion – but we must be vigilant.

References

Afshar, H (1998) *Islam and Feminisms: an Iranian case-study*, Macmillan: London and St Martin's Press: New York.

Becher, J (ed.) (1991) *Women, Religion and Sexuality: studies on the impact of religious teachings on women*, World Council of Churches: Geneva.

Edwards, M and Sen, G (1999) 'NGOs, Social Change and the Transformation of Human Relationship: A 21st-century Civic Agenda', paper delivered at the Third International NGO Conference, University of Birmingham, UK, 10-13 January 1999.

Francis, P (1999) 'Globalisation and the Human Spirit: Buddhism and social engagement in Thailand', paper delivered at the Third International NGO Conference, University of Birmingham, UK, 10-13 January 1999.

Hansen, KT (1992) *African Encounters with Domesticity*, Rutgers: New Jersey.

Hawley, JS (ed.) (1994) *Fundamentalism and Gender*, Oxford University Press.

Joseph, A (ed.) (1990) *Through the Devil's Gateway: women, religion and taboo*, SPCK: London.

Longwe, SH (1995) 'Institutional opposition to gender-sensitive development: learning to answer back' in *Gender and Development* Vol. 3, No. 1, Oxfam GB: Oxford.

Mukhopadhyay, M (1995) 'Gender relations, development and culture' in Gender and Development Vol 3 no 1, Oxfam GB:Oxford

Porter, F, Smyth, I, and Sweetman, C (eds.) (1999) *Gender Works: Oxfam experience in policy and practice*, Oxfam GB: Oxford.

Ver Beek, KA (forthcoming) 'Spirituality: a development taboo' in *Development in Practice*, Oxfam GB: Oxford.

Reconciling Islam and feminism

Iman Hashim

Islam is often represented as a religion which denigrates women and limits their freedom. However, many scholars have found evidence in Islamic texts which is supportive of women's rights. Whereas Western concepts of feminism are often resisted as foreign and subversive of Muslim culture, arguments for women's equality from within Islam hold a lot of potential for feminists.

Feminists have tended to regard religion as just another of the sources of women's subordination, citing the manner in which women are often represented as subordinated in religious texts, and the frequency with which religion is used to justify and maintain men's dominant position in society (White 1992). Although these charges are levelled at all the major religions, Islam in particular has a reputation for being 'anti-woman' and for supporting a segregated social system where women are economically and politically marginalised.

Many Muslim women and men disagree with such a view, arguing that the Qur'an provides significant rights for women, which are often far more wide-reaching than the rights which secular legal systems provide for a state's female citizens. However, many Muslims are frequently mistrustful of feminism, because they see the feminist emphasis on equal rights as at odds with the Islamic notion of the complementarity of the sexes, and the specific roles and rights laid down for men and women, which they believe reflect their particular strengths and weaknesses (Afshar 1997).

Given these differences, it is somewhat unsurprising that Western feminists have not drawn upon Islamic texts when addressing gender inequalities in Muslim societies. In this article, however, I shall question such a position and argue that, for a variety of reasons, feminists may have more to lose than to gain from maintaining such a view.

Islam and the West

The first issue that must be addressed when considering the relationship between feminism and Islam is the historical relationship between Islamic and Western societies, as this has important ramifications for both Muslim women in general and feminists, Muslim or otherwise. This history is best described as one of conflict and mistrust, stemming from the real – and perceived – economic, political, and theological threats which Islamic and Western social systems have posed to each other. This tense relationship has continued, and even intensified, in the modern era, particularly since the 1970s, when the world began to witness something of an Islamic revival (Esposito 1992).

8

In the West, the enmity between these ideological positions is reflected in the representations of Islam which conjure up images of totalitarian states and irrational believers – violent, oppressive men and powerless, submissive women. This misrepresentation in the West has been a means of supporting and maintaining its position of dominance (Said 1978). Stories of the poor treatment of Muslim women were used by colonial powers (Ahmed 1992) and missionaries (Kandiyoti 1991) to discredit Islam, and 'the custom of veiling and the position of women in Muslim societies became, in their rhetoric, the proof of the inferiority of Islam and the justification of their efforts to undermine Muslim religion and society' (Ahmed 1992, 236-7). The result has been that as a defensive reaction, the Islamist position regarding women has become even more retrogressive and reactionary, to the extent that Afkhami, an academic and political activist, goes so far as to suggest that 'contemporary Islamist regimes are most lucidly identified, and differentiated from other regimes, by the position they assign to women in the family and in society' (Afkhami 1995, 1). Any intervention targeted at women, or any attempt by feminists to change the position of Muslim women from a position which totally rejects Islam, results in accusations of cultural imperialism or neo-imperialism (Kandiyoti 1991).

Reasons for feminist engagement with Islam

Currently, accusations of neo-imperialism are most visible in the context of development work, as it is in this arena that most feminist thought is 'delivered' to Muslim countries. For example, Rashiduzzaman (1997) reports on increasing attacks on non-governmental organisations (NGOs) by Islamist groups in Bangladesh, who see these NGOs as cultural adversaries, and part of the more general 'Western' project of domination. Such views can all too easily be used by opponents of women's rights to rally opposition to feminist

ideas (An-Na'im 1995), while local participants in a development project lay themselves open to accusations of betrayal (Kandiyoti 1991). These considerations provide the first reason for feminist engagement with Islam.

A further problem with a feminist position which totally rejects Islam is that this does not take into account the importance of Islam for women. Women do not tend to report religion as the source of constraints placed on them (Shaheed 1995); moreover, religion often gives women a sense of identity and belonging, not to mention psychological support. This makes it almost impossible for the average Muslim woman to retain her identity and position in society, were she to reject religious laws and customs (Shaheed 1995), especially because 'in the absence of alternatives it is unlikely that women will abandon precisely those structures that provide them with solace and support' (ibid., 92). Therefore, secularist arguments will have little or no appeal to Muslim women. Many women are, moreover, interpreting religion in their own way as a means of responding to oppression. For example, practices such as the Zar (spirit possession) act as legitimate opportunities for the oppressed to 'let off steam' (Kandiyoti 1998), and some argue that women also use them to 'form friendships and patron-client relationships, to promote economic transactions and to offer and gain services' (Constantinides 1978, in Hale 1996, 234).

It is therefore highly relevant for development practitioners to take into consideration the relevance of local beliefs. The importance of making interventions appropriate to the indigenous context has recently been recognised in development thinking as central to the effectiveness of planning and implementing development work (Stirrat and Henkel 1996). From this perspective, it is important that development practitioners and/or feminists address Islam, not only to avoid inappropriate interventions which might alienate the communities in which they work, but also to be aware of existing social structures and norms which might promote more effective implementation.

Addressing women's interests through the Qur'an

There is a significant gap between what the Qur'an says and the manner in which its teachings are practised[1] (Ali 1993); and the Qur'an provides rights for women which can immediately be drawn upon to improve women's circumstances. Those issues that women usually do complain about, such as lack of freedom to make decisions for themselves, or the inability to earn an income (for example, Shaheed 1995), can all be addressed by referring to the Qur'an. I am not suggesting that knowledge of one's rights according to the Qur'an can be sufficient for changing social relations. However, women can and have used these to great effect. Much of the women's movement in the West has focused not only on bringing gender inequalities to light, but on formalising issues in legislation. Yet here in Islam, we as women have rights which are stated in a source considered to be divine, and consequently much harder to refute, but which we do not draw upon.

For example, Goetz and Gupta's (1994) study on credit provided to women in rural Bangladesh finds that a significant proportion of these loans are directly invested by their male relatives. Women borrowers thus bear the responsibility for repayment without necessarily benefiting from the loan. They argue that women's access to credit is important, but limited as a strategy for women's empowerment, given the lack of their control over these loans. However, a verse in the Qur'an (4:34) is frequently interpreted as giving women complete control over their own income and property, while men should be responsible for maintaining their female relatives. If education on such a right was incorporated into the consciousness-raising components of credit programmes, it might prove an effective means of preventing the misappropriation of women's property, given that Muslims consider its source indisputable[2].

Promoting women's knowledge of their Islamic rights becomes even more important when one considers the frequency with which politico-religious groups cite so-called Islamic laws applied in other Muslim countries to support their own demands for more stringent or discriminatory 'Islamic' law (Shaheed 1995), or the manner in which Muslims are often misled by self-ordained Muslim divines (Bhatty 1993). Given their levels of illiteracy, particularly women's illiteracy, and the fact that the Qur'an is often still read in Arabic, poor Muslims are particularly vulnerable to this kind of manipulation.

Indeed, the historical misrepresentation of Islam has had profound and far-reaching consequences for women. The most glaring cases are the practices of veiling and *purdah* (seclusion). Many argue that these have no foundation in the Qur'an, but demonstrate the manner in which patriarchy has circumvented the Qur'an's essentially egalitarian message (Mernissi in El-Solh and Mabro 1994). It is worth exploring this argument in greater detail, as a means of illustrating how Islam has been used as a method of controlling women. This points out the necessity to engage with Islam from a position of knowing, and to ensure that Muslim women have access to this knowledge.

The example of veiling and purdah

There are four verses in the Qur'an that are used to justify veiling and/or *purdah* (seclusion). They are open to a number of interpretations, as is evidenced from the enormous variation in whether practice veiling and/or *purdah* or not. A Lebanese scholar, who undertook an extensive study of the various interpretations, states that she found over 10 interpretations – 'none of them in harmony or even agreement with the others' (Zin al-Din 1928, in Shabaan 1995, 65). Two verses are addressed to women in general, and two to the Prophets' wives (Shabaan 1995). However, their interpretation as commandments to veiling is challenged by Islamic scholars from a variety of perspectives[3].

The two verses addressed to the Prophet Mohamed's wives are 33:33 and 33:53, exhorting them to 'stay quietly in your houses and make not a dazzling display, like that of the former Times of Ignorance'; and stating: 'And when ye ask (his ladies) for anything ye want, ask them from before a screen: that makes for greater purity for your hearts and for theirs'. These verses often form the basis for arguments in favour of veiling and seclusion; other Islamic scholars argue that such interpretations are inaccurate, particularly in light of the fact that women in general, as well as the Prophet's wives – particularly Khadija – were often publicly visible, and independent, wealthy, and active in their own right (Stowasser 1987). Such interpreters suggest that rather than an injunction to cover up and stay behind closed doors the first of these verses is an injunction against parading finery, in keeping with the Islamic ethos of not coveting or valuing material goods (Ali 1993). Similarly, the second of these verses can be interpreted, even by non-feminists, as a mark of respect for the Prophet's wives rather than a demand for their seclusion (Ali 1936). Even if one disagrees with these interpretations, the Qur'an states clearly that the Prophet's wives are not like other women (33:32); consequently, the verses directed at them can be argued not to apply to women as a group (Stowasser 1987).

The two verses that refer to women in general have been similarly challenged. These state: 'O Prophet! Tell Thy wives and daughters, and the believing women, that they should cast their outer garments over their persons (when abroad) that is most convenient that they should be known as such and not molested' (33:59); 'And say to the believing women that they should lower their gaze and guard their modesty; that they should not display their beauty and orna-ments except what (must ordinarily) appear thereof; that they should draw their veils over their bosoms and not display their beauty…' (24:31). The first of these, however, must be read in context: Ali (1936) explains that the object was not to restrict the liberty of women, but to signify their identity as Muslims, and thus protect them from harm in the insecure

conditions in Medina at the time. It requires a significant stretch of the imagination to interpret these verses as meaning that women should be totally covered or confined to their homes. Furthermore, if women were to be entirely covered, there would be no need to ask men to also lower their gaze and guard their modesty (Shabaan 1995). Similarly, it has been argued that, as it is compulsory for women not to cover their faces during pilgrimage and prayer, two of the central five pillars of Islam, then it would be nonsensical to do so ordinarily (Al-Ghazali in Shabaan 1995). Women's public visibility during the Prophet Mohamed's own life-time undermines the arguments for seclusion. Finally, if women were to be in seclusion and thus not actively engaged in earning an income, what would be the purpose of the verse that states 'to men is allotted what they earn and to women what they earn' (4:32) (Abu Shiqa in Shabaan 1995, 75)?

Although there are many problems with the representation of veiling and *purdah* in Western, and early feminist, literature, which has helped to perpetuate an image of Muslim women as victims, and denied the diversity of meaning and practice associated with this tradition, it is generally accepted that these practices contribute to women's subordination. They frequently restrict women's movements, affecting their access to production and economic autonomy, and increasing their dependence on men (Gardner 1994). Veiling has become an institutionalised aspect of Islam in many Muslim societies, which serves to illustrate both the importance of a knowledge of Qur'anic injunctions, and the need to challenge patriarchal interpretations which are used as a justification for practices which maintain an inequitable status quo. As for *purdah*, while interpretations of the Qur'an which have obliged women to remain within the household have not always precluded Muslim women from earning a living – a well-known example in the gender and development literature is of the lace-makers of Narsapur – the degree to which they have control over these earnings is questionable, given their inevitable marginalisation from institutions which could represent them, and dependency on male relations for the marketing of goods (Mies 1982).

Reconciling Islam and feminism by returning to the Qur'an

Despite the various advantages of drawing upon Islam when addressing women's position in Muslim societies, some might argue that Islam is ultimately a religion which provides men with status, control, and authority over women, and which supports a system of inequitable gender relations, and that one should not attempt to tackle women's subordination through a religion which is, in the final analysis, inegalitarian. However, of recent years activists have made efforts to reinterpret the Islamic sources, suggesting that these can be read as fully supportive of equal human rights for all.

These arguments are complex. Put simply, this strategy involves returning to the Qur'an, and conducting a study of the value system presented in the holy book. The first point these activists make is that we must look to the Qur'an, not the other Islamic sources – the *hadith*, the *sunna*, and the *shariah* – for guidance. The *hadith* and *sunna* are commentaries on the Prophet's life, tradition, and sayings, while the *shariah* refers to laws created in the first centuries after the Prophet's lifetime (An-Na'im 1995). In other words, all these sources are the outcome of human understandings of the Qur'an, which are influenced by the context in which they were conceived. As this was an era which was organised hierarchically and patriarchally, these sources inevitably reflect this reality, and the identity of the commentators, who were overwhelmingly men (Afkhami 1997).

On this basis, these theorists argue that we need to return to the Qur'an as the true source of guidance, as this alone is the word of God. The theorists also identify two aspects of Qur'anic instruction: the socio-economic and the ethical-religious categories. While women's status is inferior to men's in the former category, they are full equals in the latter. Muslim reformists argue that the difference between men and women in the socio-economic sphere belongs to the category of social relations (*mu'amalat*), which are subject to change, whereas their moral and religious equality belongs to the category of religious duties towards God (*ibadat*), which are immutable. The moral and religious equality of men and women represents the highest expression of the value of equality and therefore constitutes the most important aspect of Islamic instruction. Since men and women are full equals in creation, in mind, and in their spiritual and moral obligation (i.e., the category of *ibadat*), there is no justification for inequalities between the sexes (Shabaan 1995; Stowasser 1987).

Although one might dismiss these arguments as an intellectual exercise with little practical use for women, feminist theologians are using these reinterpretations to challenge and amend civil legal codes. For instance, Iranian feminists have concentrated on one particular verse of the Qur'an (4:34), part of which reads 'Men are the protectors of and maintainers of women because God has given the one more (strength) than the other, and because they support them from their means'. Feminist theologians in Iran argue that as the only distinction made between Muslims in the Qur'an is that between the pious and the impious (49:13), the word taken to mean 'protectors and providers' in the verse above is more appropriately interpreted as 'initiator in affairs'. Since social transformations such as women's education and employment, as well as their participation in politics, economics, and even warfare, have occurred, the Iranian civil code, which gives husbands the status of head of household and establishes unequal conjugal rights on the basis of this verse, is no longer appropriate. Not only is it inappropriate but it is un-Islamic, as the Qur'an makes no distinction on the basis of gender (Afary 1997).

A further tactic used by Iranian women is to concede to the notion of complementarity, but to emphasise that women are not 'forever mothers and that the public domain too is in great need of women's specific talents and valuable contributions' (Afshar 1997, 764). Iranian women also highlight that complementarity refers to both men's and women's roles in creating social units and in sustaining growth and development. Women have demanded that the skills involved in the care and management of home and family be both recognised and valued, and that the government help them fulfil these roles as well as facilitate their return to the workplace. In this way, a number of limited measures to improve the position of the women in the labour market have been achieved, including paid maternity leave, shorter working hours, and an earlier retirement age, in recognition of women's double burden of unpaid domestic work and paid employment (ibid.).

Overall, by drawing upon an Islamic discourse, Iranian activists have had a measure of success in improving women's rights and social position.

Conclusion

I have argued that there are significant reasons why feminists might benefit from drawing upon Islam when attempting to address the particular subordination of Muslim women. At an individual level, Muslim women will be unlikely to subscribe to a Western notion of feminism, which would mean abandoning beliefs which they have a commitment to and which provide them with mechanisms to deal with and resist the oppression they face. Moreover, the Qur'an lays down significant rights for women, of which they are often unaware, but which can be drawn upon to address and improve their circumstances. At the political level, women's exclusion from religion in the past has resulted in the dominance of patriarchal interpretations of the Qur'an. It is only from a position of knowledge that women can claim their rights and contest patriarchal interpretations of Islam.

Having said this, I do not wish to present an over-simplistic or over-optimistic view of the potential for women's emancipation as a result of either knowledge of their rights or feminist reinterpretations of the Qur'an. This strategy is, of course, insufficient in and of itself. Many Muslim women are politically and economically marginalised, and this in itself prevents them from claiming their rights, let alone from using theological arguments to do so. In this sense, reinterpretation of the Islamic texts from a feminist perspective remains an academic and intellectual exercise, and it is primarily more affluent and educated women who are able both to engage in this debate and to benefit from its argument. Moreover, women's experiences of Islam are myriad, and their subordination is not only based in so-called Islamic practices. Consequently, one cannot prescribe some form of universal formula to overcome the constraints Muslim women face, and strategies adopted must respond to these contextual constraints.

Incorporating the study of rights accorded to women in Islam into the awareness-raising and educational components of development interventions could be very effective in improving women's lives. Addressing these issues from within an Islamic perspective would prevent opportunistic accusations of cultural imperialism (intended to prevent feminism from entering an Islamic culture), and would be more likely to appeal to Muslim women. Although egalitarian reinterpretations of the Qur'an are currently relatively marginalised and limited in their scope, Muslim women (and men) are actively working not only to reinterpret the Qur'an, but also to educate the political elite and provide them with new interpretations of the sacred texts which can be used as a basis for legislation. Activists are also making efforts to mobilise grassroots support for these activities and to establish a dialogue between people at the grassroots and national and international decision-makers, in order to ensure the dissemination and adoption of these interpretations (Afkhami 1997).

Speaking as a woman born into a predominantly Muslim family and community, and having undertaken a study into gender and Islam, I now recognise the ways in which Islam is frequently misrepresented (deliberately or otherwise). Having studied what the Qur'an actually states, I am now in a position to oppose patriarchal interpretations and to challenge others when debates are foreclosed on the basis of my gender. This, for me, is remarkably liberatory; but it is easy to get carried away by one's personal experience. I am a Northern-based, privileged woman who is relatively untouched by these interpretations of Islam. I can only imagine the constraints facing women in other socio-geographical locations. It is important to be aware of the problems of advocating the dissemination and adoption of egalitarian interpretations, and not to underestimate the dangers involved in contesting patriarchal interpretations of Islam – witness the plight of Taslima Nasreen or the recent death threats levelled at Nawal el Sadaawa, the Egyptian feminist. However, the mere fact that this does arouse such strong reactions, I would suggest, is testimony to the potentially significant ramifications of such a strategy.

Iman Hashim is a sociologist and anthropologist currently working at the International Labour Office before returning to the University of Sussex to undertake her DPhil. Contact details: 7-86, BIT, 4 Route de Morillons, 1211 Geneva, Switzerland. Tel. +41 (22) 799 8893. Fax +41 (22) 799 6349. E-mail: hashim@ilo.ch or I.M.Hashim@sussex.ac.uk

Bibliography

Afary, J (1997) 'The War Against Feminism in the name of the Almighty: Making Sense of Gender and Muslim Fundamentalism' in *New Left Review*, No. 224, pp. 89-110.

Afkhami, M (ed.) (1995) *Faith and Freedom: Women's Human Rights in the Muslim World*, I. B. Taurus & Co.: London and New York.

Afkhami, M (1997) 'Promoting Women's Rights in the Muslim World' in *Journal of Democracy*, Vol. 8, No. 1, pp. 157-166.

Afshar, H (1997) 'Women and Work in Iran' in *Journal of Political Studies*, Vol. 45, No. 1, pp. 755-67.

Ahmed, L (1992) *Women and Gender in Islam: Historical Roots of a Modern Debate*, Yale University Press: New Haven and London.

Ali, ZS (1993) 'Women in Islam: Spirit and Progress' in Siddiqi, ZA and Zuberi, AJ (eds.) *Muslim Women: Problems and Perspectives*, MD Publications: New Delhi.

An-Na'im, A (1995) 'The Dichotomy between Religious and Secular Discourse in Islamic Societies' in Afkhami, M (ed.) *Faith and Freedom: Women's Human Rights in the Muslim World*, I. B. Taurus & Co: London and New York.

Bhatty, Z (1994) 'Socio-Economic Status of Muslim Women' in *Indian Journal of Social Science*, Vol. 7, Nos. 3-4, pp. 335-40.

El-Solh, CF and Mabro, J (1994) 'Introduction: Islam and Muslim Women' in El-Solh, CF and Mabro, J (ed.) *Muslim Women's Choices: Religious Belief and Social Reality*, Berg: Providence.

Esposito, J (1992) *The Islamic Threat: Myth or Reality*, Oxford University Press: Oxford.

Gardner, K (1994) 'Purdah, Female Power and Cultural Change: A Sylheti Example' in Journal of Social Studies, No. 65, pp. 1-24.

Goetz, A-M and Gupta, RS (1996) 'Who Takes the Credit? Gender, Power, and Control Over Loan Use in Rural Credit Programmes in Bangladesh' in *World Development*, Vol. 24, No. 1.

Hale, S (1996) *Gender Politics in Sudan: Islamism, Socialism, and the State*, Westview Press: Boulder and London.

Holy Qur'an 'Translation and Commentary' by Ali, AY (1936) Islamic Propagation Centre International: Birmingham.

Kandiyoti, D (1991) 'Introduction' in Kandiyoti, D (ed.) *Women Islam and the State*, Macmillan: London.

Kandiyoti, D (1998) 'Gender, Power and Contestation: "Bargaining with Patriarchy" Revisited' in Jackson, C and Pearson, R (eds.) *Feminist Visions of Development*, Routledge: London and New York.

Mies, M (1982) *The lace makers of Narsapur : Asian housewives produce for the world market*, Zed Press: London.

Rashiduzzaman, M (1997) 'The Dichotomy of Islam and Development NGOs, Women's Development in Bangladesh' in *Contemporary South Asia*, Vol. 6, No. 3.

Said, E (1978) *Orientalism: Western Conceptions of the Orient*, Pantheon: New York.

Shabaan, B (1995) 'The Muted Voices of Women Interpreters' in M, Afkhami, (ed.) *Faith and Freedom: Women's Human Rights in the Muslim World*, I. B. Taurus & Co.: London and New York.

Shaheed, F (1995) 'Networking for Change: The Role of Women's Groups in Initiating Dialogue on Women's Issues' in Afkhami, M (ed.) *Faith and Freedom: Women's Human Rights in the Muslim World*, I. B. Taurus & Co.: London and New York.

Stirrat, R and Henkel, H (1996) 'Fundamentalism and Development', unpublished report, ODA: London.

Stowasser, BF (1987) 'Religious Ideology, Women and the Family: The Islamic Paradigm' in Stowasser, BF (ed.) *The Islamic Impulse*, Croom Helm: London and Sydney.

White, S (1992) *Arguing with the Crocodile: Gender and Class in Bangladesh*, Zed Books: London.

Notes

1 Those *ayas* considered to be the most significant to women and gender relations are listed here. However this list is by no means comprehensive. They are referenced according to the *sura* (chapter) and relevant *aya* (verse). Thus 33:25 refers to the thirty-third chapter and twenty-fifth verse of the Qur'an. All are taken from Yusuf Ali's (1936) translation of the Qur'an. *Spiritual and Moral Issues*: 2:256, 3:195, 4: 1, 4:80, 4:124 , 4:92, 6:107, 9:71, 9:72, 10:99, 16:125, 33:35, 40:40, 48:5, 57:12, 88:21, 88:22; *Marriage* 2:187, 2:221, 2:223, 4:19, 4:34, 4:4 , 5:6, 30:21, 33:52; *Divorce*: 2:229, 2:236, 2:237, 2:241, 4:20, 4:21, 4:35, 65:6, 4:130; *Polygamy*: 4:24, 4:3, 4:129; *Inheritance and Property Rights*:4:7, 4:11, 4:12; *Veiling and Purdah*: 4:32,24:30, 24:31, 33:32, 33:33, 33:53, 33:59

2 Using this argument is a relatively contentious issue, given that feminists frequently call for the equality of the sexes. To take such a position could be seen as playing into the hands of those who would argue that such an interpretation conforms to a notion of a 'weaker sex', reliant on male relatives for support. Moreover, challenging this interpretation is precisely what Iranian feminists are doing in their fight for a more equitable interpretation of the Qur'an (as discussed later). Nonetheless, for communities who do subscribe to such a conceptualisation of gender roles, this interpretation could be used to great effect.

3 Cf. Shabaan (1995) for a comprehensive discussion of this.

Christianity, development, and women's liberation

Bridget Walker

Development practitioners working for gender equity must understand the significance of religion for many women who live in poverty. Both development interventions and religion are concerned with poverty; and both have often been problematic for women. Religious faith can offer women the opportunity for liberation; but it can also encourage conformity.

Introduction

'I was active in the church throughout the 20 years of my marriage, during which I lived in constant fear ... The church was my lifeline ... It was the only place my husband allowed me to go ... but these (the church's) messages helped me stay in that relationship of fear for a long time' (quoted in Gnanadason 1997, 45).

This quotation illustrates the ambiguous nature of the support offered to women by religious institutions. For this woman, trapped in a violent relationship, the Christian church provided the only chance to associate with others and to escape temporarily from the prison of her home – yet it did not offer her liberation. On the other hand, religion has been a resource in struggles for equality and emancipation for many women. Gender and development workers must be aware of these two options – domestication and liberation – because on the one hand, religious teaching preaches women's subordination through imposing social codes regarding women's roles, behaviour, and relationships with men. On the other hand, church may also offer the only space in which women can meet.

While religion may seem remote and even irrelevant to increasing numbers of people in Britain (my own context) it is an important force in the lives of many people on other continents. It is of personal significance, providing rituals at deeply emotional moments of birth, marriage, and death. It offers opportunities for reflecting on the meaning and purpose of life, and an explanation for suffering. It prescribes codes of behaviour in the family and beyond, and provides a means of expressing a communal identity. It may shape the nature of the state, and influence the way the economy is run. On the other hand, religion offers alternatives to the dominant models of social, economic, and political development (White and Tiongco, 1997). Many Christians in Latin America have turned to the messages which liberation theology has for those living in poverty or under oppression; others, in both Americas, have embraced Christian fundamentalism.

I focus on the Christian tradition, because it is the one I know best: it has shaped the society in which I live, the communities among whom I have worked, and my own thinking as a feminist and a development worker. I shall look primarily, but not exclusively, at the tradition and legacy of the churches which emerged in the West[1] and missionised the Americas, Africa, and Asia. I shall examine briefly what these churches have to say about the nature of women, family relations, and other social institutions, and how women in the South have responded.

Christianity and 'development'

Christians have always described development in terms which go beyond conventional definitions of development as modernisation and economic growth. The papal encyclical *Populorum Progressio* (1967) claimed development as a new name for peace. A Christian Aid pamphlet[2] published in 1970 states: 'Development means growth towards wholeness: it describes the process by which individual persons and communities struggle to realise their full potential; physical and intellectual, cultural and spiritual, social and political. Thus, development is a Christian concern' (Christian Aid 1970, 5).

However, in countries of the South, development interventions have succeeded colonialism, which was influenced by the Christian missionary activities of imperial powers. Religious authority has often been allied with social, political, and economic power. As a consequence, theological doctrine has reflected establishment interests, given ideological support for the rise of capitalism, and, through missionary activity, imposed a Western world-view on the religious consciousness of other cultures. 'When white people came to South Africa, they had the Bible, and we had the land. But now we find that they have the land and we have the Bible.' (Roxanne Jordaan in King 1994, 155).

However, there have always been challenges to the religious institutions of the establishment. In Europe in the sixteenth century, movements to reform the doctrines and institutions of the Christian church claimed the word of God in the scriptures as the supreme authority, thus challenging the priestly hierarchy. The Bible became accessible to people in their own languages and their own homes. It continues to be a resource for Christians working for change today. The Jubilee 2000 Coalition[3] is an international movement of churches and development agencies which bases its messages about the cancellation of Third World debt on the Biblical imperative of justice for the poor. In Africa, Christians have sought an authentic, 'de-colonised' theology, while in Asia the struggle for human rights has focused the thinking of Christian men and women. The church in the Philippines was divided during the years of repression: the establishment supported the state, while many individual Protestants and Catholics joined Muslims and Marxists in the people's struggle for change (Duremdes 1989, 38). Throughout Latin America, a theology has emerged which explicitly names itself a theology of liberation.[4] In situations where there was no freedom to speak directly about the political and economic situation in Latin America, it was still possible to tell stories from the Bible. People immediately understood the messages of the Old Testament prophets who condemned unjust landlords, the sharp practice of profiteers, and the corruption of the courts; they identified with the gospel narratives of the New Testament in which the sick are healed, the hungry fed, outcasts are befriended, and which presents a vision of a kingdom of justice and love. Liberation theology has influenced current development thinking about participation and empowerment (Eade 1997). I return to consider women's relationship to liberation theology in the next section.

Christianity, women, and social institutions

In this section, I examine the opportunities and constraints which exist for women in the tradition of mainstream Christianity regarding their sexuality and family life – at community level, within the church itself and in convent life, in the economy, and at the wider national and international levels.

Sexuality and the family

The churches have often interpreted human nature in a manner that is profoundly damaging to women. In particular, the control of female sexuality is of concern to patriarchal society: this control is expressed in many religious and cultural forms. Christianity may be used to deprive women of autonomy over their own bodies, for example, through the prohibition of abortion (as in the case where the Pope, head of the Roman Catholic church, advised the Archbishop of Sarajevo that the women who had been raped had a duty to bear the children thus conceived (Gnanadason 1997). The negative impact of this attitude not only affects women at the level of their personal and social relations, but also shapes the legislation of states which have a Christian tradition which makes women subordinated, second-class citizens.

The fact that women often seek support from the churches in family matters is ironic, considering their record. Aruna Gnanadason, of the World Council of Churches, has commented: 'Our concerns have been the sanctity of the family, reconciliation, restoring marriages, when often the first need is for an end to violence, for safety for women and children, and for justice for the oppressed' (Gnanadason 1997, 43).

From 1988 to 1998, Christian churches took part in the Ecumenical Decade of Churches in Solidarity with Women, which was designed to keep alive the concerns of the UN Women's Decade (1975-85). One of its activities was a four-year process of visiting all members of the World Council of Churches (WCC) and analysing the findings from these visits. The teams (usually two women, two men, and a WCC staff member) met church leaders, members of congregations, students and teachers of theology. The WCC's main topics of research mirrored the priorities of the UN Women's Decade: violence against women;

women's full participation in the life of the church; the global economic crisis and its effects on women; racism and xenophobia and their effects on women.

More than 200 people were engaged in making the visits. Each team wrote its own report, which was then forwarded to the church concerned. *Living letters*, published by the WCC in 1997, is a digest of these reports with extensive quotations from the discussions[5]. In *Living letters*, the authors comment that the dominant model of the family they encountered was a traditional, hierarchical, and patriarchal one, in which women played a submissive role.

A different view of women's role in family and society can sometimes be conveyed effectively through discussions of gender issues in development. At a gender-training workshop in which I participated, organised by Oxfam GB in Kenya some years ago, we discussed women's and men's roles in the home and in agriculture, and their different workloads. The values underlying Oxfam's work in development were discussed, such as the need for everyone's participation – men's and women's – in planning processes and in making decision which would affect their lives. There was a lively discussion of these issues, with much use by participants of scriptural references to support their points of view. A proverb which suggested that beating and love were connected was firmly repudiated by a participant who quoted the Bible. Love, she said, is patient and kind.[6] In the closing session, a church leader who had at the outset quoted scriptural references to support male authority, and who had claimed that the equality of women and men was 'against God and nature', said thoughtfully that he needed to re-think the way in which his church was governed, and his role in it. Perhaps, he said, he should not be doing everything himself.

Mercy Oduyoye, a theologian from Ghana, comments caustically: 'African men sing "Viva" when people talk about racial and class exploitation, but they can hang you if you dare talk about sexism. They say African culture legitimates it and, if they are Christians, sections of the Bible seal it for them' (King, 1994, 66). Women become dangerous when they question patriarchal models in this way, for this is to question the foundation of institutions as broad as the state and as intimate as the family. Christian feminists may be regarded by men and women alike as destructive of relationships, the family and all that is sacred.

Organisation and leadership in the churches

Throughout most of history, the Christian churches have been run by men, and leadership is still largely in men's hands. Yet, paradoxically, many churches have also provided the opportunity for women to meet, discuss, organise, and learn new skills. Rigoberta Menchu, the Guatemalan revolutionary leader, describes in her autobiography how, at the age of 12, she became a lay preacher, and how the church provided her with the opportunity to develop leadership qualities and to organise (Burgos Debray 1984). However, she criticises the way in which the priests encouraged her people to remain passive and accept the status quo. Menchu calls for a church of the people, organised by them, and reflecting their experience of hunger and oppression. She sees this church as more than a building or an organisational structure; it is a real change within people. This change should also address the relations between women and men and the 'machismo' (male attitude of domination) which she likens to a sickness. Ofelia Ortega from Cuba[7] argues that the contribution of Latin American women is essential for the maturity of liberation theology. Its message of good news and deliverance from bondage for the poor must reflect poor women's experience and needs. In the Christian Base Communities[8] of Latin America, women are represented in significant numbers – the structure of organisation is more participatory, and less formal, clerical, and hierarchical than in the traditional church.

Here women are free to read and reflect on the Bible from their own perspective and to relate it to their own lives.

Religious orders: an alternative model of community

The convent may at first glance seem an unlikely launch pad for women's liberation. Yet some women in Europe struggling for the right to vote in the nineteenth century looked back on the convents of the past and claimed that 400 years earlier, these had been communities in which women could develop their potential and serve society. Religious women today suggest that religious communities represent an alternative 'corporate' model in social structures which remain dominated by men, and which still position women in family or kinship groups, and identify them as daughters, wives, and mothers.

The church in the market place

While the members of religious orders usually make vows of poverty, Christian religious foundations often hold substantial company shares to provide income. In Britain, Canada and the United States, religious women have played a key role in shareholder action[9], challenging transnational corporations (TNCs) to take ethical considerations into account in their operations in countries of the South. This challenge is one form of working in solidarity with those women and men struggling for the liberation of Third World countries. Sharon Ruiz Duremdes from the Philippines, writing in Women in a Changing World (WCC Women's Unit 1989), sees this as an important way of 'doing theology' for women in the countries of the North.

International networking for change in the churches

The WCC has supported a range of global initiatives focusing on women, of which the Ecumenical Decade of Churches in Solidarity with Women has been one of the most far-reaching, challenging member churches and providing a voice for women of faith. Theirs is a voice of critical solidarity. *Living letters* (WCC 1997) makes a series of recommendations to churches. One of them argues that the churches should denounce violence against women, regardless of whether it is culturally sanctioned; another that they should recognise the links between sexism and racism, and combat them at the centre of church life. Another recommendation is that economic injustice against women should be addressed through development programmes and advocacy concerning the root causes of women's poverty. Economic justice must also be practised in the way churches are run, through equal opportunities and equal pay. The forms and substance of religious practice need to be re-examined in the light of women's experience and perspective, and their need for liberation.

The voices of women

What are women themselves saying about religion today? In many social contexts, 'feminism' remains a suspect and threatening concept, and many women would reject the title of feminist, while nevertheless following the first principle of feminist theology – being faithful to their own experience. There are a number of positions which I would like to categorise, rather crudely, as follows: re-affirming the faith; reclaiming it; reforming it; and rejecting it.

Re-affirming the faith
Women in the Orthodox churches have argued that it is possible to be faithful to church tradition, and work for change within it. The Living Letters initiative found that, in Russia, the specificity of the roles of women and men means that, in the parishes, the priest has a mostly spiritual role, whereas the administrative decisions are taken by women, who run the parish council. Women are active in social and work and in religious education; they feel that their contribution is recognised and appreciated (WCC 1997).

At times of personal or political upheaval, women may choose to reaffirm their religious affiliation. This may be a source of solace, or offer a form of identity; it may be a conservative or a radical move, or it may, paradoxically, contain elements of both. For example, women and men who supported the Catholic church in Poland in the days of the Cold War were participating in religious practice which presented a radical challenge to the Marxist government of the day, yet the Polish church remained deeply conservative in its attitude to women. 'Resistance theology', like 'resistance politics', has seldom reflected women's interests until challenged to do so by women in the movements.

Reclaiming the faith
It has been important for many women of different traditions of faith, including Christianity, to return to the roots of religious belief, in order to analyse how some aspects have been given prominence by religious institutions, while others have been ignored. They argue that men have used religion to serve their patriarchal purposes, but that there is a more woman-friendly tradition to be reclaimed: the early Christians lived in an egalitarian community of women and men,[10] and women held positions of leadership. Christian women have looked for liberating models in the Bible: Deborah the Judge and Esther the Queen in the Old Testament, and the women in the community around Jesus in the New Testament. Mary, so often presented as an impossible ideal of the woman as virgin and mother, is reclaimed as the strong 'female face' of the faith, proclaiming the reversal of the established order: 'he [i.e., God] has pulled down princes from their thrones and exalted the lowly; the hungry he has filled with good things, and the rich sent empty away' (Luke 1, 52-23). The Bible offers a diversity of images of God, from which the church has selected mainly masculine terms; feminist theologians argue that to name God only in terms of father, warrior, king, and lord is to limit our understanding of the divine-human relationship. Ofelia Ortega

suggests that this task of reclaiming also is important for men, whose spirituality she sees as having been damaged by the distortion of biblical revelation (WCC 1989).

Reforming the faith

Many feminist theologians argue that reclaiming the faith is not enough, because religions arise in specific historical contexts, and are formed by the political and economic forces and social attitudes of the time. Therefore, the codes and practices developed at one time need to be reformed for a changed social context. Movements for the ordination of women have used this argument. Feminist theology takes as its starting point the search for women's identity, grounded in women's own experience, rather than in the forms imposed by a patriarchal culture. This leads to personal and social transformation.

Women theologians of the South have also stressed the necessity of addressing the inheritance of cultural and spiritual imperialism from the missionary endeavours which brought Christianity to continents including Africa. Teresa Hinga, from Kenya, sees Christ as an ambivalent figure for African women: he is both conqueror and liberator. She suggests that it was the latter perception of Christ and the 'emancipatory impulses' within missionary Christianity which led to a positive response from Africans. Hinga quotes the example of women among the Kamba of Kenya, who tried to break away from unsatisfactory marriages or harsh parental control by seeking refuge with the Africa Inland Mission, a Protestant mission in that area (Hinga, 1994).

Another important focus for feminist theologians has been that of language: the translation of the Bible, and the words of the liturgy. Gnanadason argues that the images of God in Western Christianity are based on the 'social norms and gender role specifics in that culture's national, ecclesiastical, business and family level' (Gnanadason 1989, 29). Drawing on examples from India, she points out the need to move beyond the conven-

tional masculine image of God, asserting that God can be depicted in alternative, and female forms; and that new and diverse models of God should be developed to include the experience of all peoples.

Rejecting the faith of the fathers

Many women reject organised religion because they see it as part and parcel of a profoundly contaminating patriarchy, built on, and maintained by, violence. The Christian churches are judged to have been complicit in the violence of colonialism in the past, and genocide in this century. But women from formerly-colonised countries, whose consciousness has been formed in a Christian tradition, continue to seek means of articulation of their spiritual experience, often drawing on their Christian heritage. Oduyoye looks at the tradition of independent Christian movements which have emerged in opposition to the racism and ethnocentrism of Euro-Americans on the African continent. At some churches, African Christian women have tapped into the primal religious sources of their communities, for example through the healing ministry of a prophetess.

Conclusion

At the beginning of this article, I stated that those concerned with social development and social justice should analyse the role of religious institutions in the lives of women, and understand their relationship to them. I have outlined how the traditions of the Christian church have often demeaned women, but have also, paradoxically, supported them within the parameters of existing social structures. Through a brief discussion of how women have claimed liberation from a perspective grounded in their faith, I have examined different perspectives on the extent to which forms of Christianity offer scope for women's liberation or oppression. Women's continued critique of Christianity demonstrates that their relationship with it is more often one of engagement than rejection. Development workers concerned with the struggle against poverty and its causes, and with improving the quality of life for all, must listen to what women are saying about the spiritual as well as the material dimension of their lives.

Bridget Walker is currently a member of the Strategic Planning and Evaluation team of Oxfam GB. She was previously an Adviser in Oxfam's Gender and Development Unit. Contact details: Oxfam GB, 274 Banbury Rd, Oxford OX2 7 DZ. Fax +44 (1865) 312 600; e-mail bwalker@oxfam.org.uk

References

Burgos Debray, E (ed.) (1984) *I, Rigoberta Menchu*, Verso: London.

Duremdes ST (1989) ' Women in Theology: Philippine Perspectives' in *Women in a Changing World*, Issue 28, May 1989, WCC:Geneva.

Eade D (1998) *Capacity Building: An approach to people-centred development*, Oxfam GB: Oxford.

Gnanadason, A (1997) *No Longer a Secret: The Church and Violence against Women*, WCC Press: Geneva.

Gutierrez, G (1983) *The Power of the Poor in History*, SCM: London.

Hinga T (1994) 'Jesus Christ and the Liberation of Women in Africa' in King, Ursula (ed.) *Feminist Theology from the Third World*, SPCK: London.

IDOC and the Commission of the Churches on International Affairs: *Human Rights: A Challenge to Theology*, Rome.

Jordaan R in King, Ursula (ed.) (1994) *Feminist Theology from the Third World*, SPCK: London.

Ortega, Ofelia (1995) *Women's Visions: Theological Reflection, Celebration, Action*, WCC: Geneva.

Taylor, Michael (1990) *Good for the Poor: Christian Ethics and World Development*, Mowbray: London.

The Jerusalem Bible (1986) Darton, Longman and Tod: London.

White, S and Tiongco, R (1997) *Doing Theology and Development*, Saint Andrew Press: Edinburgh.

WCC Women's Unit (1989) 'Women doing Theology and Sharing Spirituality' in *Women in a Changing World*, Issue 28, May 1989, WCC: Geneva.

Notes

1 The Christian church was established as the religion of the Roman Empire by the end of the fourth century. It split into two major groups: the Eastern (Orthodox) church, and the Western church with the Bishop of Rome (the Roman Catholic Pope) at its head. The Roman Catholic church was subsequently split by reform movements which led to the establishment of Protestant churches. (There are also smaller churches with an ancient history, such as the Nestorians, the Copts (Egypt), and the Ethiopian church. All these, like the Eastern Orthodox church, generally did not expand through missionary activity in the same way as the Western churches.)

2 Jay, Eric (1970) *World Development and the Bible*, Christian Aid: London.

3 Jubilee 2000 is an international movement of development agencies and church bodies calling for the cancellation of the unpayable debts of the poorest countries by the year 2000. For a description of the Year of Jubilee, when debts are written off, see Leviticus 25, 8-17.

4 At a meeting in Medellin in 1968, the Roman Catholic Bishops of Latin America denounced the unjust maintenance of wealth by a few at the expense of the majority of citizens, and placed themselves firmly on the side of the poor, according to the Gospel's imperative to bring good news to the poor, proclaim liberty to the captives, and to set free the downtrodden (Luke 4, 18-19). Liberation theology started from the position of the oppressed and the poor seeking liberation. The expression 'liberation theology' was used by the Peruvian theologian Gustavo Gutierrez.

5 The booklet was also the result of a team effort and has no single author. The foreword is written by Nicole Fischer-Duchable, the WCC consultant to the Mid Decade Process.

6 1 Corinthians 13, 10-12.

7 'Women doing Theology and Sharing Spirituality', p.10-11 in *Women in a Changing World*, Issue 28, May 1989, WCC: Geneva.

8 The Christian Base Communities are a feature of liberation theology in practice. Grassroots groups within the Catholic church meet to reflect on the Bible and the teachings of Jesus as these relate to their own lives. They have provided an opportunity for women to organise, to participate in decision making, and to enjoy a freedom they may not have at home.

9 Shareholder action bodies such as the Interfaith Committee on Corporate Responsibility in the USA, and the Ecumenical Council for Corporate Responsibility in the UK, encourage churches and religious foundations with investments to raise ethical questions at annual general shareholder meetings, and to engage in dialogue about the companies' operations in the South.

10 Acts 4, 32-35; see also Gnanadason (WCC 1989, p.30).

Conflict and compliance:

Christianity and the occult in horticultural exporting

Catherine S. Dolan[1]

The introduction of new export crops in the early 1990s upset the customary division of labour between men and women in Meru District, Kenya, and led to conflict over land, labour, and income. Women's workload increased; their earnings did not. They responded by turning to 'born-again' Christianity for support, and by resorting to traditional witchcraft to regain control.

Religion and witchcraft are often perceived as peripheral to developmental objectives. At best, they are considered interesting phenomena of social life; at worst, they are viewed as relics of societies out of step with the modern world. Development practitioners tend to view religion as a static feature of culture, with little relevance to the success of development interventions (Mukhopadhyay 1995). Drawing on research conducted from 1994-96 and briefly in 1998, this article challenges this assumption: in Meru District, Kenya, the introduction of export horticulture has generated conflict over land, labour, and income, and women use witchcraft and Christianity to mitigate intra-household struggles over income from export crops. Women are responding to the erosion of their rights in ways that may appear paradoxical: some undergo Christian conversion, while others bewitch and poison their husbands. Some do both. These practices simultaneously comply with male authority, and resist it.

While the region has a long history of export-oriented agriculture (coffee and tea), it had become one of the largest French bean-producing areas in Kenya by the 1990s. This has had a profound effect on female farmers. Prior to the introduction of French beans, women's land (conventionally very small plots) was used to grow vegetables for household consumption and for sale at local markets. In response to pressure for agricultural diversification to supply the expanding European market for 'gourmet' vegetables, horticulture – historically a female domain – has been rapidly intensified, commoditised, and, in many cases, appropriated by men. The profitability of French beans grown for the export market is raising the stakes in horticultural production; men usurp either the land allocated for, or the income derived from, French bean production. The customary division of labour by crop and gender is currently undergoing a sea-change, as tensions escalate over male and female property rights and women's contributions to household subsistence.

The spiritual domain has become a principal forum through which struggles over land and labour are expressed; these struggles can undermine the developmental objectives of export horticulture.

Global food networks and gender relations

Until the 1980s, food consumption patterns of urban populations in the West were limited by the seasonal availability of locally grown fresh produce. In contrast, today agro-food chains deliver fresh fruits and vegetables from all over the world to Western consumers. These are grown in the so-called new agricultural countries (NACs). Sub-Saharan Africa has a comparative advantage in the production of export horticultural commodities, because of its good climatic conditions, geographic proximity to European markets, preferential trade agreements, and, most importantly, an abundance of cheap labour (Barrett et al. 1997).

Agricultural diversification into high-value, labour-intensive commodities such as French beans ('non-traditional' exports) are central to IMF/ World Bank programmes to reduce poverty through export-led growth (World Bank 1981, 1995). In particular, agricultural diversification strategies are promoted as a vehicle to enhance gender equity through increased female employment (e.g., Chilean *temporeras* and Mexican *maquiladoras*). Yet research on the social implications of growing non-traditional exports (NTEs) has been largely restricted to Latin America (Collins 1995; Thrupp 1995; Barrientos 1997; Bee and Vogel 1997) with little attention awarded to Africa, where NTEs account for a growing share of women's economic activity. Horticultural exports (principally cut flowers and vegetables) are now the fastest growing agricultural sectors in many African economies (Zimbabwe, Zambia, and Kenya), and a critical source of foreign exchange, particularly with the recent decline in revenues from traditional export crops.

Labour utilisation and income distribution

When policy practitioners promote horticultural exports to raise rural incomes, they invariably fail to consider the amount of labour a household must invest to secure a profit. The quality standards that most horticultural crops must meet – governing their texture, fragrance, colour, weight, and shape – make them highly labour-intensive, and resistant to mechanisation. Kenya's most widely grown export vegetables – snow peas and French beans – are extremely labour-intensive, demanding 600 and 500 labour days per hectare respectively (Carter et al. 1996; Little 1994). It is mainly women who are compelled to invest more time in specific tasks such as planting and weeding, yet their work remains categorised as unpaid labour. In fact, the economic benefits of growing French beans and other horticultural export crops are predicated upon the unpaid labour of women and children.

Several studies (Schroeder 1996; Carney and Watts 1990; Mackintosh 1989; Mbilinyi 1988) have recorded the cultural norms which govern the division of labour and control of resources between women and men, and which affect the extent to which women can receive benefits from export production. My research confirms that in Meru, biases in men's favour regarding the distribution of land, labour, and income undermine the potential of French bean production to provide developmental benefits for women and children.

First, the exacting labour and time constraints on women involved in export-crop production directly affect their ability to participate in other activities. Women are expected to meet the family's subsistence needs, and to augment household income through the sale of local crops. While men do work on French beans, for the most part they perform tasks of relatively low labour intensity such as clearing fields and applying fertiliser. Furthermore, although men have more spare time to allocate to French bean production than women, there has been no adjustment of the gender division of labour in existing activities between husband and wife. This has eroded women's capacity to fulfil their households' subsistence requirements. Women who are able to retain their proceeds from French bean sales are choosing to allocate more labour to the cultivation of French beans than of subsistence crops. Men resent the withdrawal of female labour from subsistence crops (unless they are given the money earned from the cultivation of the French beans), and have challenged the right of women to use vegetable plots for French bean cultivation. Furthermore, because men are garnering significant amounts of money from export cultivation, they are less likely to work on their wives' plots. As a result, women are compelled to hire labour to perform tasks that were formerly covered by reciprocal labour exchanges.

Second, the gendered nature of property rights also directly affects the benefits women derive from French bean production. In Kenya, women's access to land is mediated by their marital status, their household position, and decisions made about land use by male relatives. As in much of Africa, men have the right to control the proceeds from the crops grown on female plots. Over 33 per cent of the women interviewed claimed that their husbands had either compelled them to grow French beans on their usufruct plots[2], or retracted their rights to them completely. This violates conjugal norms, because not only are French beans cash crops (the earnings from which traditionally go to men throughout Africa) but they are also vegetable crops (the income from which women have the rights to in customary law).

Third, although French bean production has created a new mechanism for income generation, there is a wide disparity in the distribution of income from it between men and women. My research showed that women perform 72 per cent of the labour for French beans, and obtain 38 per cent of the income. Even where women receive the returns from their labour, they are often compelled to contribute this cash to household expenditures that would, until now, have been their husband's responsibility. Finally, the profitability of French beans has incited men to appropriate the income, which customarily has been under women's control.

Conflicts between husbands and wives over the allocation of income from French beans are commonplace and often escalate into household violence. As one female interviewee claimed: 'The crops that result in wife-beating today is coffee and tea, because they are termed as a man's crop. Many husbands misuse money from these crops and when asked they beat their wives. *Michiri* (French beans) are also cause for beating. When we try to keep our money, our husband asks where it is. If we don't give it to him we are beaten. These crops cause us many problems'.

Because family labour, specifically women's labour, is the fundamental source of labour for French bean production, the success of export horticulture rests on sound cooperation between husband and wife. Traditional social structures which used to deal with marital strife have been eroded, so that women now tu0rn to alternative means of resolving conflict.

Gender and the supernatural

In Meru, the spiritual domain has become the principal area in which gender-based conflicts over crops, property rights, and labour allocation are expressed. Both Christianity and witchcraft reflect the nature of social and economic relations, and hence are useful idioms for interpreting issues of power and domination in rural life. While the presence of witchcraft appears at odds with Christian revivalism, both represent ways of expressing discontent with prevailing social norms, and offer women strategies to reclaim autonomy and security within their households.

Christianity
Africa today cannot be considered apart from the presence of Christianity: a presence which, a couple of generations ago could still be dismissed by some as of marginal importance, and a mere subsidiary aspect of colonialism (Hasting 1990:208). There are currently over 25 distinct Christian denom-

inations in Central Imenti, 43 churches, and new churches are built each month. Women participate in church groups that meet once a week to practise singing, organise church events, and to discuss both personal and religious matters. While women generally perform duties that replicate their responsibilities at home such as cooking and cleaning, most women I spoke to claimed that they would rather clean the church than their own home, because they were doing it for God, not for their husbands. They told me that they look forward to their weekly gatherings as a time of freedom and an opportunity to gossip, laugh, and seek respite from the routine of daily labour and the problems at home.

The Kenyan state's conception of gender roles is so intertwined with the Christianity proselytised by village leaders that it is nearly impossible to separate Christian values from social life. Young girls are socialised from a very early age to be good Christian girls – obedient, submissive, and accommodating – to attract a suitable man for marriage. One interviewee told me that a good woman (*mwekuru umwega* in Kimeru) 'obeys her husband and does not speak rudely to him. She welcomes the guests and does all the work her husband asks her to do.' Her sentiments are widely echoed by other women in Meru, who agree that a *mwekuru umwega* 'does not quarrel with her husband, does not speak badly about her husband and obeys him always'. In fact, some women said that they deserve punishment for failing to meet the Christian standards of a 'good' wife. This linkage between religion and virtue in is reinforced by the Kimeru term *kimatha*, which connotes a bad woman who neglects God, and her husband and children.

Yet despite this, for many women in Meru and elsewhere, the church presents a means to escape the confines of their marriage, since direct challenges to male authority entail too high a cost. In Meru, becoming 'saved' involves witnessing to Christ, and acknowledging Jesus as a personal saviour. The crusade toward being 'born again' has become increasingly widespread through Central Imenti during the last decade. The phenomenon of 'saved' individuals originated among the Methodists and the East African Revivalists in 1947-48 and the numbers continue to rise: my sample of 200 randomly selected households included 95 per cent 'saved' women in comparison to 35 per cent 'saved' men. In fact, I never met a woman who was not 'saved'. In Meru, being born again is now synonymous with being a good Christian and I was encouraged to profess my own conversion, or risk being perceived as an agent of the devil.

Being 'saved' is extremely important to these women: most could recount the moment when they turned over their lives to God. Most women claimed that they have turned to God to bear with the perpetual marital and intra-household struggles they experience; a principal problem is disagreement over French bean income. Many told me that being 'saved' enabled them to handle the difficulties of their marriage; one told me it was 'the only solution' to the powerlessness she experienced in daily life. The transformative power of becoming 'saved' is a significant part of a woman's identity, and offers her not only a means of coping with her life, but also an opportunity to join with other women who share her experience.

Becoming 'saved' is most prevalent among women who have a high stake in the stability of the household system, and few alternatives for autonomy. Women who do not conform to the 'patriarchal bargain'[3] (Kandiyoti 1988) are vulnerable to insecurity, poverty, and landlessness. This is particularly true for women who have no male sons to provide them with land, and thus have no source of protection outside of their marriage.

While female Christian conversion can be seen as capitulation, I view it as a strategy designed to foster self-determination while maintaining an outward appearance of Christian compliance. In order to avoid sanctions from men and the wider community, women act within the parameters of prevailing social norms (von Bulow 1991).

Witchcraft

Witchcraft is not merely a 'traditional relic' of tribal societies, but is woven into the fabric of modern life. Expressions of the occult are well documented in situations of economic change, where the introduction of new resources exacerbates social differentiation and increases struggles for power and control (Geshiere 1997; Goheen 1996; Drucker Brown 1993). Further, theories suggest that women are predominantly associated with the occult because they are socially marginalised, which is expressed in various symbolic forms such as spirit possession, sorcery, and witchcraft (Ardener 1970; Drucker-Brown 1993; Ong 1987).

In Kenya, witchcraft is blamed for illness, death, and natural catastrophe, and people may be lynched and mobbed because of their perceived connections with the occult. Throughout the country, accusations and counter-accusations of witchcraft exacerbate community tensions and contribute to growing violence. In 1994, President Daniel Arap Moi took a stand against occult practices, following reports that devil worshipping and witchcraft were infiltrating educational and government institutions, and widespread claims that his administration was avoiding an investigation because some of its members, as well as opposition figures, were involved in a satanic cult (Wachira 1994). Kenyan politicians are known to exploit people's paranoia by invoking satanism to win votes. For example, during the 1992 elections, a Democratic Party (DP) politician sprinkled a potion in the ballot boxes professing that individuals who failed to vote DP would be haunted by 'the bottle' (*The Nation*, 24 May 1995).

Fear of the occult is pervasive in Meru; witchcraft is inscribed in the consciousness of the area and is expressed in a repertoire of stories, for example: 'I know a girl, Tabitha from Kibirichia, who left home with an unknown woman to be employed by a woman at Maua. But instead of them going to Maua they went to Thika. She was stripped naked and kept in the house. She was told to write a letter home and tell them of her incoming death. She wrote home and the parents received the news with shock. They hurriedly got the police and they saved the girl. The girl later told them of how people were taken there and eaten by other people ... That people there were living with the devil'.

In Meru, the changing balance of power between men and women in domestic, economic, and political spheres has led to the emergence of witchcraft accusations by men against women. In the 1920s, colonial administrators had become intent on banishing the issue of witchcraft from Meru, contending that the District's development was being impeded by the persistence of 'superstition', and the perpetuation of 'secret societies'. In particular, officials were concerned over the reports of women's *kiamas* (societies), where women practised witchcraft to ensure the obedience of their husbands. The women's intent was said to be not so much to kill their husbands as 'to force them to seek alternatives, preferably by providing ... gifts sufficient to induce removal of the curse' (Fadiman 1993:160). A spate of women either giving their husbands *kagweria* – a substance that induces psychosis and leaves control of the household to the wife – or poisoning their husbands to death, was recorded early in this century, and reappeared in the 1970s. *Kagweria*, a liquid taken from certain trees, is mixed with a bouquet of sedative drugs.

Today, women in Meru practise many forms of witchcraft (both sorcery and bewitching)[4] which are widely used to secure power and autonomy within their marriage. *Kagweria* is purchased from knowledgeable women, and its use is rapidly being taught to Meru women by women in other districts. In Githongo Location, a 35-year-old woman administered the potion to her husband, aged 39. The man not only suffered from common dementia as a result, but also experienced a severe psychotic state. Following his hospitalisation, his wife was implicated. Under investigation, she disclosed that there was a group of four women who had perfected the recipe and were distributing it to other women. One interviewee described women's involvement in the following way:

'Women buy [kagweria] from other women who are old. Kagweria is a charm given secretly by women to their men that changes men's mental ability to a worse state. Once a man is fed with kagweria, he stops giving orders to his woman and therefore the woman becomes the head of the family. This [use] has increased because we are dealing away with our traditional customs. Before, the clan would intervene in husband and wife cases. Now the clan doesn't do much for us, so we get a solution for ourselves. Men don't respect their wives or they are not all that faithful like before. They still love with other women and this annoys the wives. Most women do not want to accept that a woman should always be under a man, like they tell us. We are envious of the progressing way of other women who have freedom. A way to have freedom is to give kagweria ... [and obtain] power over the wealth, especially from the good crops.'

One particular interviewee knew of seven cases of bewitching within the last two years, all provoked due to interfamilial struggles over French bean income. Churches regularly organise women's seminars to preach against the practice and to teach women how to ameliorate household struggles through Christian service. Despite this, many of the same women who publicly espouse the tenets of Christianity privately employ witchcraft.

Baraza (public assemblies) are frequently organised by village politicians to mitigate male anxiety regarding women's increased utilisation of witchcraft and poisoning, and to lecture women on norms of female obedience. One particular case concerned the poisoning of a village man, whose wife claimed that he refused to allocate any French bean income to her. A village woman described the incident in the following way:

'In Katheri, a wife worked with her daughters to bewitch her husband and take all the wealth. The man was forced to stay in the house for three weeks with vomiting and diarrhoea. The church is taking the duty to preach against bewitching now. In June, the Four Square preachers held a crusade and prayed and pointed out one of the women from Kiithe village who has been supplying kagweria. They chastised her. But usually these women aren't found because witchcraft can only be carried out at night. It is very secretive ... Only talked about ... Never seen with the eyes'.

In Meru, Kenya, witchcraft reflects women's struggles for power in an arena in which they have been customarily denied a more direct vehicle for asserting their aims. The growing prevalence of witchcraft is one consequence of the expansion of French bean production and its exacerbating effect on intra-household disparities. As men's individual ambition has overridden their customary social responsibilities (through the appropriation of women's incomes and usufruct rights to land), women have developed strategies to reclaim autonomy and security within their households.

As the number of witchcraft cases in Meru District mounts, men are terrified. The rise in the number of baraza and village meetings to lecture women on female obedience is testimony to men's growing fear of female aggression. Men have no reason to believe that their wife will be an exception to the recent movement. As Geshiere contends (1994, 325), 'witchcraft is indeed the dark side of kinship: it reflects the frightening notion that there is hidden aggression and violence where there should be only trust and solidarity'. Thus, as long as men were not jeopardising women's access to resources in the female domain, women largely allowed public political power to remain in men's hands. But as men have encroached upon the income derived from French beans, a crop culturally coded as female, the boundaries and meanings of gender relationships have changed (Goheen 1996). In this situation, women's resistance cannot be overlooked, because the viability of export-promotion strategies for development depends upon women's willing participation.

It is widely agreed in gender and development circles that an understanding of how resources are distributed within the household is critical to the success of policy interventions (Kabeer 1995; Goetz and Sen Gupta 1994). Yet development practitioners continue to overlook how cultural factors influence the outcome of agricultural diversification initiatives. In this case, the failure to acknowledge cultural dynamics has not only undermined the purported aims of gender equity, but also worsened women's well-being, and ultimately men's security.

Catherine Dolan is a Visiting Lecturer at the School of Oriental and African Studies, London, and a Research Officer at the Institute of Development Studies, University of Sussex, Brighton BN1 9RE. Phone: +44 (1273) 606 261. Fax: +44 (1273) 621 202. E-mail: c.dolan@ids.ac.uk

Notes

1 I would like to thank Fulbright, the Social Science Research Council, and the National Science Foundation for their generous support of this research. I also extend my appreciation to the University of North Carolina and the Centre of African Studies, SOAS, for supporting the write-up of my thesis, on which this paper is based.
2 Usufruct land is property under male control which women have the rights both to cultivate and to retain the income derived from that production.
3 This phrase refers to women's conformity to social norms – such as being a good wife and mother – in a male-dominated society, in return for rewards such as social acceptance and status.
4 In daily discourse there is little difference between sorcery and witchcraft. In Kiswahili, both are described as uchawi, although witches are perceived to have an ascribed status, whereas sorcerers achieve their status through study in the application of substances (Brain 1992).

References

Apter, A (1993) 'Attinga Revisited: Yoruba Witchcraft and the Cocoa Economy, 1950-1951' in Comaroff, J and Comaroff, J (eds.) *Modernity and its Malcontents: Ritual and Power in Postcolonial Africa*, University of Chicago Press.

Ardener, E (1970) 'Witchcraft, Economics and the Continuity of Belief' in Douglas, M (ed.) *Witchcraft Confessions and Accusations*, Tavistock: London.

Barrett, H, Browne, A, Ilbery, B, Jackson, G, and Binns, T (1997) 'Prospects for Horticultural Exports Under Trade Liberalisation in Adjusting African Economies', report submitted to the Department for International Development.

Barrientos, S (1997) 'The Hidden Ingredient: Female Labour in Chilean Fruit Exports' in *Bulletin of Latin American Research*, 16(1):71-81.

Bee, A and Vogel, I (1997) 'Temporerars and Household Relations: Seasonal Employment in Chile's Agro-Export Sector' in *Bulletin of Latin American Research* 16(1):83-95.

Brain, J (1982) 'Witchcraft and Development' in *African Affairs*, 81(324):371-84.

Carney, J and Watts, M (1990) 'Manufacturing Dissent: Work, Gender, and the Politics of Meaning in a Peasant Society', *Africa* 60(2):207-241.

Carter, M, Barnham, BL, and Mesbah, D (1996) 'Agricultural Export Booms and the Rural Poor in Chile, Guatemala and Paraguay' in *Latin American Research Review*, 31(1):7-33.

Collins, J, 1995, 'Gender and Cheap Labor in Agriculture', in McMichael, P, (ed.) *Food and Agrarian Orders in the World-Economy*, Praeger: Westport.

Drucker-Brown, S (1993) 'Mamprusi Witchcraft, Subversion and Changing Gender Relations' in *Africa* (63):531-549.

Fadiman, J (1993) *When We Began There Were Witchmen, An Oral History from Mt. Kenya*, University of California Press: Berkeley.

Geschiere, P and Fisiy, C (1994)

'Domesticating Personal Violence: Witchcraft, Courts and Confessions in Cameroon' in *Africa* 64(3):323-341.

Geshier, P (1997) The Modernity of Witchcraft, University of Virginia Press: Charlottesville.

Goetz, AM and Sen Gupta, R (1996) 'Who Take the Credit: Gender, Power and Control over Loan Use in Rural Credit Programmes in Bangladesh' in *World Development*, 24(4).

Goheen, M, (1996) *Men Own the Fields: Women Own the Crops: Gender and Power in the Cameroon Grassfields*, University of Wisconsin Press: Madison.

Hastings, A (1990) 'Christianity in Africa' in King, U (ed.) *Turning Points in Religious Studies*, T. and T. Clark: Edinburgh.

Kabeer, N (1995) 'Necessary, Sufficient or Irrelevant? Women, Wages and Intra-household Power Relations in Urban Bangladesh', IDS Working Paper #25, Institute of Development Studies: Brighton.

Kandiyoti, D (1988) 'Bargaining with Patriarchy' in *Gender and Society* 2(3).

Little, P (1994) 'Contract Farming and the Development Question' in Little, P and Watts, M (eds.) *Living Under Contract: Contract Farming and Agrarian Transformation in Sub-Saharan Africa*, University of Wisconsin Press: Madison.

Mackintosh, M (1989) *Gender, Class and Rural Transition: Agribusiness and the Food Crisis in Senegal*, Zed Books: London.

Mbilinyi, M (1988) 'Agribusiness and Women Peasants in Tanzania' in *Development and Change*, 19(4):549-583.

Mukhopadhyay, M (1995) 'Gender Relations, Development Practice and "Culture"' in *Gender and Development*, Vol. 3, No. 1, Oxfam GB: Oxford.

Ong, A (1987) *Spirits of Resistance and Capitalist Discipline: Factory Women in Malaysia*, SUNY Press: Albany.

Schroeder, R (1996) 'Gone to Second Husbands: Marital Metaphors and Conjugal Contracts in The Gambia's Female Garden Sector' in *Canadian Journal of African Studies*, 30(1):69-87.

Thrupp, L (1995) *Bittersweet Harvests for Global Supermarkets: Challenges in Latin America's Agricultural Boom*, World Resources Institute: Washington.

von Bulow, D (1991) 'Transgressing Gender Boundaries: Kipsigis Women in Kenya', CDR Project Paper 91.3, Centre of Development Research: Copenhagen.

Wachira, C, 'Probe into Devil Worshipping Spawns Controversy', Interpress Service, 1 November 1994.

World Bank (1981) 'Towards Accelerated Development in Sub-Saharan Africa', Washington DC.

World Bank (1995) 'Kenya Poverty Assessment', Population and Human Resources Division, Eastern Africa Department, Washington DC.

No time to worship the serpent deities:

Women, economic change, and religion in north-western Nepal

Rebecca Saul

Why do the inhabitants of one village in north-western Nepal still follow Buddhist customs, when religious rituals have all but died out in the neighbouring village? Rebecca Saul outlines how the evolution of a competitive tourist economy has affected local social structures and women's roles, as well as women's attitude to the spiritual realm.

This article is a tentative exploration of the changing relationships between lay women, and the spiritual realm, in two ethnic Tibetan communities in Barabong in north-western Nepal. It focuses on the ways in which economic and social change has affected women's often unseen and unrecognised spiritual roles within both the household and the community; and on how these roles have in their turn influenced the course of such change. I am drawing on 15 months of doctoral research in Nepal, which set out to look at how individuals in two communities faced, initiated, and resisted change. I found that in the world view of the inhabitants of Kag and Dzong, the social, physical, and spiritual realms are not distinct, but intricately and inextricably connected.

What is the link between gender and development and this research? First, development interventions are themselves part of a wider process of constant change, and the impact of change, be it the product of 'development', political upheaval, economic re-orientation, or other forces, has related consequences for gender relations within households and communities. The second

link is my contention that the Buddhist concept of interconnection – the belief that changes in one realm have a profound impact on the other realms – is, in essence, a concept which should underpin development. Just as Buddhists believe that performing a religious ritual in the physical realm appeases or propitiates a deity in the spiritual realm, so we, as development practitioners and academics, are aware that an irrigation project affects not only agricultural productivity but can also have an impact on the division of labour, land rights, social dynamics, and so on.

Background

Mustang District is located in north-western Nepal, and shares its northern border with Tibet. No motorable roads extend into Mustang but the district capital, Jomsom, can be reached on foot from the city of Pokhara in mid-western Nepal – a five-day walk up into the Kali Gandaki River Gorge – or by a short plane journey. From Jomsom northwards, the local people are described anthropologically as ethnic Tibetans, and within Nepal as Bhote. The people of Baragong in lower Mustang, who are the focus of this article, speak a local Tibetan dialect (referred to as Southern Mustang Tibetan) and officially follow various Buddhist sects, of which Sakya is currently the predominant one. Marriage practices, social ranking, religious rituals, and general cosmological understandings are similar to those found in areas of Tibet, and among other ethnic Tibetan groups in the Himalayas.

Kag

Kag village has a population of about 360 people in 63 households. It is a minor administrative centre for the area of Baragong, boasting a health post, a police checkpoint, several development offices, and a post office. In addition to all of these 'modern' amenities, a large Buddhist monastery and the remains of an impressive castle suggest that Kag was an important religious, economic, and administrative centre. Today, with a dozen tourist lodges and several camp sites, Kag is one of the most popular tourist destinations for trekkers journeying to and from the Muktinath Valley and north into upper Mustang.

In general, many of the people of Kag village have embraced 'modernisation': it was the first village in the area to receive electricity, the first to respond to the arrival of tourists by building guest houses, and also the first village to abandon several of the more important village rituals in Baragong.

Dzong

From Kag, several thousand feet up the Muktinath Valley, lies Dzong village. Dzong is described both by the people who live there, and by other villagers in the area, as a place where the old ways are kept alive. The population of Dzong is slightly smaller than that of Kag, with about 250 inhabitants. Because Dzong is located within a semi-restricted area, tourists can travel to the village for a day, but are not permitted to spend the night there. Dzong does not have a police post, health centre, or post office.

While many of the inhabitants of Dzong participate fully in a market economy, and have embraced the ideology and practice of

development along 'modern' lines, Dzong remains – in the words of people in Dzong and other villages in Baragong – 'true to the old ways'. Rituals and practices which have been abandoned in Kag and other villages in the area not only survive in Dzong, but are seen by many Dzongba[1] as the raison d'être of being Dzongba, the things that define them as Dzongba.

Living in Baragong

Like many of the peoples who populate the high mountain regions of Nepal, the Baragongba[2] have a three-pronged subsistence strategy of agriculture, pastoralism, and trade. Kag and Dzong, like most villages in Baragong, are socially stratified. Although there are numerous ways in which the social status of individuals and households can be judged, the main social groupings are those of noble, commoner, and sub-commoner. The middle of these three 'grades' is the most numerous and, in some villages, the only strata. These hierarchical grades had far more importance in the past than they do today.

In Baragong, as in other ethnic Tibetan societies, there exists an ideal form of household organisation which is linked to ideas concerning landholding, inheritance, residence, and marriage, as well as being located in the domains of symbolism and ritual (Phylactou 1989). Although households vary greatly in composition and economic standing, the ideal, and the most common structure for commoners and sub-commoners[3], is the corporate estate household, called *drongba*. A *drongba* estate is collectively owned by an extended family group. At the core of the *drongba* household is a patriline (group of men related by blood): a man and his wife, or a group of brothers and their wife, the father(s) and mother of the man or brothers, and their children.

Historically, being part of a *drongba* meant high status. *Drongba* households paid tax and performed labour for the noble households, and as a result gained certain privileges, such as first access to irrigation water. *Drongba* households also were the backbone of religious life in the communities of Baragong. Until recently, the wives of male *drongba* heads, called *kimpamo*, had certain rights, including the right to attend the mid-winter festival of *Dokyap*. While noble women rank above all other women in the village including the *kimpamo*, they had no special ritual roles or responsibilities. During the festival, only *kimpamo* women danced the traditional dances in the monastery grounds and the village square. Apart from the obvious honours bestowed upon these women, they were generally more active in village life, and more highly respected than non-*kimpamo* women.

Gender relations

Women in Baragong have significant domestic and civic power. Women are resource-holders – they inherit and own land, and runt their own businesses – and decision-makers – they choose their marriage partners, obtain divorces, control their own fertility, and participate in village-level politics.

Marital forms
Baragongba households are ideally based on the Tibetan 'monomarital principle': in each generation of a family, one and only one marriage can be contracted. In theory, the practice of fraternal polyandry (brothers sharing one wife), ensures that the family inheritance is kept within one household, since all the sons remain in the household into which they were born and share the inheritance, rather than allowing inheritance by one child only. If there are no sons, a daughter inherits the estate and brings her husband into the household; it is also possible, but quite rare, for her to marry polygynously, to share a husband with her younger sister or sisters. Although her husband is seen as a male household head, it is the woman who is recognised as the estate holder. In practice, Baragongba women who inherit their own patrimonial estate have more say in household affairs than those who share their husbands' patrimony.

Decision-making in the household
The household in Baragong is a corporate unit. All money, land, and household goods (except dowry goods, which are the wife's property) are jointly owned by the husband(s) and wife. Husbands should not dispose of property without their wives' consent; nor should wives without their husbands'. Couples who are apart because of business make independent day-to-day decisions. According to couples interviewed, (and my own observations confirmed this), power relations between husband and wife are relatively equally balanced. Couples stated that this depended more on personality than gender. The ideal is for disputes to be talked through, and a solution agreed upon mutually. Indeed, the power of the head of household is narrowly limited: all household members – even the children – are involved in forming opinions and in executing decisions. While the eldest brother still has the highest status in the home and the community as household head, within the household he cannot overrule unilaterally the wishes of any other household member (see Levine 1980, 287).

Gender division of labour
The division of labour between the sexes is generally relaxed: both men and women farm, herd, trade, and practice business. Women tend to work harder than men, however, as they have primary responsibility for running the household, cooking, collecting water and firewood, looking after children, and performing many of the more laborious agricultural tasks such as weeding and processing grain. There are few hard-and-fast-rules, however, and each household manages its workload differently, depending on its labour resources.

However, it is true that, as a result of their relatively heavier domestic workload, women tend to have fewer social responsibilities outside the home. Women often told me that because meetings are called at night they cannot attend – they must cook the evening meal and care for small children.

Similarly, meetings in distant villages are difficult for them to attend because of child-care and domestic responsibilities. It is usually men who attend meetings as representatives of their households, and it is men who hold the positions of 'headman' and 'assistant headman' in the village. With the integration of Baragong into the political system of Nepal, men's political roles have been strengthened; women rarely hold positions of power on the new 'village development committees' (VDCs) or at the district level.

Spirituality and the changing role of women

In Baragong, women have always been integral to the spiritual maintenance of the household and the community. However, while women in the village of Dzong continue to play an important part in the spiritual life of their households and the community, the importance of women's spiritual role in Kag has diminished. Why this difference between the two communities? In order to answer this question, we must look more closely at how the lives of women in Kag and Dzong differ. I will discuss three major changes to women's roles and status brought about by changes in land-holding, tourism, and development.

Land-holding

First, and perhaps most importantly, the system of *drongba* estates in Kag was disbanded several years ago. This means that all people within the village have the same rights and responsibilities. There are no ritual roles, or political offices, that are open only to heads of *drongba* households. In Dzong, however, the titles of *chuktwa* (male household head) and *kimpano* still exist, and ritual, though not administrative, importance is attached to them. Men from all households in Dzong can hold the offices of headman and assistant headman, but only male and female heads of estate-holding households can participate in certain religious festivals and retreats, such as *Dokyap*.

In Kag, disbanding the *drongba* estates has meant that *kimpamo* women play a greatly reduced role in the ritual life of the village. When they do participate, they often do so alongside women from households which, in the past, were not *drongba* households. Former *kimpamo* told me that they see their ritual labour as a burden which keeps them from other, more prestigious economic activities, rather than as an honour bestowed upon them because of their status. These other, more lucrative, economic activities are tourism and other income-generating activities.

The impact of tourism

Baragong was opened to foreign trekkers in 1974. By the late 1980s, it was attracting more than 30,000 tourists every year. In Kag, tourism is an important part of the village economy; in comparison, Dzong has no tourist economy. While tourists visit year-round, the peak period – September to November – coincides with the harvesting and processing of buckwheat and the planting of barley and wheat, as well as with the large regional harvest festival held in Muktinath. The second most popular time to trek in the Annapurna region is in the spring: a time of reunion, local archery festivals, communal work, and preparation for the harvest. Running a tourist lodge denies the household the labour of at least one member during periods when their contribution is most needed, and further limits both the social and spiritual roles of these household members.

The first tourist lodge in Kag was built in 1976; by 1995 there were ten, and a further two planned. It is primarily women who run lodges. Male and female lodge-owners cited several reasons for this: cooking, cleaning, and hospitality are tasks typically taken on by women, and thus local people feel that women are naturally more capable of running lodges. Second, it is generally women who stay in the village year-round, and hence they tend to take on the primary responsibility for the least seasonal economic activities. Third, women are judged able to look after small children and run lodges simultaneously.

However, women who run lodges have less free time to engage in community rituals, festivals, and monastic retreats. Pema Dolkar, a woman lodge owner in Kag, complained that she often 'felt like a prisoner' in her own home: '... I would like to go to Yartung [a harvest festival in the neighbouring community of Muktinath] in the autumn, but I have not been now for five years because there have been so many trekkers. Sometimes it is so busy that I cannot even go to Tse chu [a village ritual on the tenth day of each month] and have to send someone else from the household instead' (personal communication, 1995).

While many female lodge owners find that their movements beyond the village are restricted, tourism and business have both enabled and encouraged men (and non-lodge owning women) to spend longer periods away from the village. Whereas in the past women played an important role in both regional trade and the salt-grain trade between Nepal and Tibet, women who have the responsibility of running a lodge rarely participate in business outside of the village.

Women who run lodges also tend to visit other households in the village less often, and participate less in the sharing of food which is so common between kin, neighbours, and friends. While it is still customary for lodge owners to offer tea to neighbours and friends without charge, the sharing of vegetables and other desirable foods now bypasses the lodges. As one woman, whose female cousin runs a lodge, commented: 'Why would my sister [cousin] give spinach to me when she could sell it to the tourists for money? We used to share food between our households all the time here [in Kag], but now many people keep things to themselves so that they can make money.'

People also say that the Buddhist ethic of hospitality has suffered since the advent of tourism. The following tale, told throughout Baragong, illustrates this point. 'There was a woman ... who set up a travellers' rest house a little way up the Thorong La [a frequently travelled pass between Baragong and the neighbouring district of Manang]. She knew that people coming from Manang, tourists and locals, would be thirsty and need a drink so it was a good business idea. But this woman – *man kalo cha*! [black soul or heart] – she would not even give away one glass of water. Local people should always receive one glass of tea free, even in a lodge; but she would even charge for water! She was very greedy and made much money ... After she died, about two or three years ago, her soul did not find the path [to 'heaven', where souls are weighed to determine their next incarnation]. She still wanders this world, haunting and possessing people. She has possessed ... [a certain woman from Dzong], as well as Baragongba in Kathmandu and Assam ...' (personal communication, 1996).

The impact of 'development'

With the opening of Baragong to tourists, 'development' was not far behind. Development ideology and practice in Kag and Dzong have proceeded in very different directions. Villagers in both communities have radically different views of what development is and should be at the village level.

There are stories of failed projects and lack of local participation in Kag. I heard divergent views of development between the younger and older generations. While younger people adhere to the bottom-up model of development held in Dzong, older people in Kag are oriented towards dependence on the outside. This idea of development as a top-down redistribution of resources from the state, sees development as a gift which 'has or has not come' and the role of villagers as passive recipients in this process (Clarke undated). One woman in Kag stated: 'I do not know the names of any of the development projects here, only the police office and the office that my son works with [ACAP]. I don't know what he does, something with trees ... Some office people came and planted some trees, but no one has watered them and most have died. ... I don't know what will happen to the trees after they have grown, whether the development people will sell them, or whether they will even be used by the Kagpa … Up to now, ACAP has done nothing but make garbage tips. They make tourists sign their names when they arrive in Kag'. Some of the accountability for failed projects must, of course, lie with the development projects themselves.

One old Kagpa woman expressed the dissonance between old ideas of 'goodness' and the ideas held by those who wish to bring development to the village: 'In the old days, we used to drink water right out of the Dzong River. The water out of the river is very good for you. Some people still drink from it [even though there is a clean water project]. We old people say that walking through the river makes the water *choko* [clean], not *jutho* [polluted]. We did not hear that the river water was bad for us before the Nepalis and development came! Mountain water is colder and tastier.'

Many Kagpa feel that development in their village has a bad track record because people are too busy with their own work and there are too many poor people: 'If there was enough money in the village, people could cooperate and do their own development.' Many of the meetings called by project staff to discuss the village's future development were attended only by lodge-owners; non-lodge-owners said they felt that development was for tourists, rather than for villagers. According to NGO staff, this low level of interest has led to many projects pulling out of Kag. During group discussions, interviews, and in casual conversations, villagers listed a number of reasons for this lack of interest in development projects. Lodge-owners rarely cooperate with each other, and because of their high social and economic status, few other villagers are willing to participate in community projects. Those who had enough money to install solar power for showers do not want electricity for the whole village, because then all lodges would be able to provide hot showers. Tourism has furthered competition rather than cooperation, especially between lodge-owners. Competition for tourist money is evident when one

passes the painted rocks along the trail leading to Kag, announcing that this lodge or that lodge has a hot shower, the tastiest apple pie, the best views.

Because most lodge-owners are women, the main conflicts are between them rather than men. The fact that gender and development literature and practice has paid much attention to women's cooperative development efforts may mean that the lack of cooperation in Kag is more noticeable than similar behaviour would be on the part of men.

Unlike the highly competitive market of tourism, business ventures in Dzong, especially those which require villagers to travel further afield to East Asia, often require the labour and financial resources of several households working together. Because of their relative isolation, and the lack of a tourist economy, the people of Dzong have had to seek support from government agencies and NGOs to improve life in the village; a key element of this relationship is that they also show commitment in the form of labour and other inputs into the projects. 'Our own village, we must build ourselves' is the development slogan heard throughout Nepal. (In the past, labour obligations were fulfilled by *drongba* households only. This has been a powerful catalyst for changing the *drongba* system to limit it to ritual activities, rather than political and economic ones.) The villagers have often worked with the people of their neighbouring villages Chongkhor and Putak in order to attract expertise, materials, and money for their projects. In sum, the Dzongba seem to have been relatively successful in making development work for them, without losing control over important village decisions; the moral ideology of equity and a commitment to 'community' have been strengthened in Dzong.

When the Dzong villagers decide that a project is needed, the village leaders sit down with the headmaster (who writes Nepali) and draft a letter to the appropriate agency. Several projects applied for in this manner have now been completed. For example, Dzong is supplied with limited electricity in the winter months by a hydro-electric project supported by the government of Nepal. Numerous small projects which the villagers initiated have been carried out with the help of development funds, including the construction of a new mill. CARE agreed to supply the necessary materials; the labour was supplied by all households.

Lay women and their spiritual roles

People's relationships with the spiritual realm are influenced by social, economic, and political change. In particular, the changing economic role of women in Kag has had profound effects on their role in religious practice.

Caring for the lu

Lu are serpent spirits which, when pleased, bring wealth and prosperity, and when angered, bring illness and misfortune.[4] Daily rituals of offering food and burning incense are enacted to propitiate the household *lu*; these are almost exclusively performed by household women. The differences in household rituals enacted in Dzong and Kag reflect what is perceived as necessary for the prosperity of the household. In Dzong, daily offerings to the serpent deities are still viewed as a vitally important part of household ritual, appeasing potentially harmful serpent deities and enlisting their aid, while in Kag prosperity is seen as less dependent on the *lu*. My Dzong landlady explained that '[I]f the *lu* ritual is not done the household will become poor, sick, and inharmonious. It will be a "dirty house".' However, in contrast, many houses in Kag do not worship *lu* or perform rituals for them any longer. A significant number of households in Kag give offerings only once a week rather than daily, as is recommended by monks and devout villagers alike. During the winter, many women in Kag do not feed the *lu* at all; they claim that the *lu* are sleeping, and therefore do not need to be appeased. This is convenient for women who leave the village during the winter for sunnier climes.

Celebrating Dokyap

The ceremony of *Dokyap* is intended to enlist the aid of benevolent Buddhist divinities and regional gods and goddesses in the protection of the village. A grandmother in Dzong told me: 'The performance of *Dokyap* pleases God. It keeps sickness and death away from people and livestock. It ensures good harvests and stops torrential rain and wind storms. For the welfare of the village, *Dokyap* must be done'.

Historically, *Dokyap* has been an extremely important event for the political and religious unity of the area and the hegemony of the local ruling class. While in Dzong the ritual has survived to this day, in Kag it declined and eventually died several decades ago.

In Dzong, *Dokyap* is still an important event: large fines are imposed on male and female *drongba* household heads who are absent from the village or who fail to participate in any of the events during the seven-day ritual. Villagers consider the festival vitally important for the preservation of local culture, the accumulation of religious merit, the expulsion of evil, and the social unity of the village.

Each day, at noon, a large drum calls the female heads of *drongba* households away from their drinking party in a house near the monastery (village women take turns hosting the party each year). Everyone gathers in the village square where the women sing and dance in traditional lines. Only women born or married into Dzong can participate; single women and widows are excluded. All of the women wear *shuli*, the ceremonial headdresses which mark them as married heads of commoner estate-holding households.

The songs sung by the women are vitally important for the efficacy of the exorcism ritual; the women singers carry the ritual effigies, and lead the procession of villagers to the monastery and to the far reaches of the village. Four masked young men chase and beat the women if they do not sing loud enough, ordering them to 'sing for the protection of the village'. The seven *Dokyap* songs can only be taught by women, and only then; they must never be sung at any other time, and should not be revealed to outsiders.

The events which preceded and followed the cessation of Kag's *Dokyap* reveal much about the importance of women in maintaining the community's spirituality, and about how and why these roles have changed. A host of social and political tensions contributed to the dissolution of *Dokyap* in Kag, and this is still the cause of much discussion and tension within the village.

The first version of events that I heard was told by a noblewoman in Kag, who has a good knowledge of history but also a vendetta against the man she names as the villain in the scenario. '*Dokyap* stopped in Kag 22 years ago, when Dhundup [not his real name] was the big man. He had two wives. His first wife wanted to leave him so she arranged for her younger sister to marry him. At this time, when he took his new wife, they did not like the *Dokyap* because we [the nobles] did. We loved it, so they went against it just out of spite … and maybe because they were embarrassed about the family situation'. The idea that Kag's *Dokyap* stressed the divisions between nobles, commoners, and subcommoners was confirmed as part of the reason why many commoners in Kag ceased to participate; villagers said that they 'did not want to beg for food from the nobles' and that 'dancing for food and drink was degrading'.

Another reason given for the decline of the ritual is the rise of economic development. As economic considerations for many villagers have begun to outweigh cultural or religious ones, people travel south in greater numbers during the winter, and thus are absent during *Dokyap*. Rice and barley, the staple foods of the festival, have begun to be seen as cash commodities: why contribute as much as 63 pounds of rice and barley (the contribution of a large household for the entire festival), when that grain could be sold for a profit? In addition, many ceremonial head-dresses used for *Dokyap* were sold to tourists in the 1970s, and the cash invested in lodges and other business ventures.

This also reveals a shift in perceptions of status. In the past, a woman who wore a particularly beautiful and richly adorned head-dress conferred status on her household. To sell a head-dress in the 1920s or 1940s would have been unthinkable, since a commoner woman without one had no real status and could not participate in communal ritual events. As modern clothing and consumer goods have replaced local dress and jewellery as signs of household prosperity, many family heirlooms have been sold.

The cessation of *Dokyap* in Kag has obvious religious implications. Singing the traditional songs is an important part of communal cleansing and accumulation of merit. In Dzong, this is still seen as so important that female heads of household who are absent from the village during *Dokyap* (usually because they have travelled south for the winter and are unable to return because of illness or heavy snows) pay a large fine, and are forbidden to participate in the ritual the following year, causing great shame for a household. In Kag, this is not the case.

Conclusion

Few Kagba women of the younger generation wish the ritual of *Dokyap* to be revived, and many of the old songs have been forgotten. What are the implications of the changes in religious observation and in economic activity in these communities for women, and for development policy and practice? A broad analysis of women's roles and women's work is needed, which includes spiritual roles and responsibilities. Do development researchers and workers include *all* dimensions of women's work in their information-gathering and policy-formulation? Do they recognise women's 'unseen' spiritual maintenance roles within their communities, which could be enhanced or undermined by development? How do women's spiritual, reproductive, productive, and community roles support (or weaken) each other? Most importantly – and this is certainly not the first time that this question has been asked – are 'economic development' and 'purchasing power' the only yardsticks by which household and community well-being should be measured?

Kag women who run lodges and spend many months away from the village are perceived by others to have neglected their social, and hence spiritual, obligations. Women's cooperative groups (so common among ethnic Tibetans in Nepal), and the practice of sharing household resources among neighbours, friends, and kinswomen, have virtually ceased in Kag. As the story of the dead lodge-owner whose soul wanders this earth illustrates, economic and social changes have consequences for the spiritual life of the Baragongba. Although the Dzongba are as successful in business as the Kagpa, and indeed travel abroad more frequently, they still consider it vitally important to be a participating member of the village. Sharing food, labour, and goods between households reinforces village solidarity, and expresses local ideas of morality and social obligations. Full social and physical participation in village life also maintains spiritual harmony within the village. Dzongba women do not seem to feel the same conflicts as Kagpa women.

For women in Kag today, there are '… paradoxes, conflicts and ambivalence surrounding the apparent contradiction between enduring religious values and current trade practice, between those who aspire toward indigenous (Buddhist) notions of 'goodness' and those whose imaginings lean toward the glamour of "life in the fast lane" …'(Watkins 1996, 6). The negative impact on individuals and the community of Kag women's neglect of traditional social and spiritual responsibilities should be weighed against the possible benefits to individual women, their households, and to women's collective status in the community of increased female economic contributions to their households. Women are gaining respect for their business acumen and their ability to earn money. My research assistant in Dzong, Khandro, offers an excellent example. In the first year of her marriage, her parents-in-law wanted Khandro to stay in the village, but her husband encouraged her to accompany him on a business trip. He stated to family and friends that 'she [his wife] is very clever and

will be of great help to me in business. Why would I marry a woman who had no head for business?' The qualities of independence and individualism are becoming more prized; however, the older generation mourn the loss of social cohesion and community spirit.

Rebecca Saul works for CARE International UK as a programme officer for South Asia and Latin America. She lived in Nepal for three years conducting research and working as a consultant, and has a PhD in Social Anthropology. Contact details: CARE International UK, 8-14 Southampton Street, London WC2E 7HA. E-mail saul@uk.care.org

References

Clarke, G (undated) 'Development (*Vikas*) in Nepal: Mana from Heaven', draft paper prepared for the Asian Studies Association Fourth Decennial Conference, Oxford.

Levine, N (1980) 'Nyinba polyandry and the allocation of paternity' in *Journal of Comparative Family Studies* 11:3.

Mumford, SR (1989) *Himalayan Dialogue: Tibetan Lamas and Gurung Shamans in Nepal*, University of Wisconsin Press.

Phylactou, M (1989) *Household Organisation and Marriage in Ladakh – Nepal Himalaya*, unpublished PhD Thesis, London School of Economics and Political Science.

Watkins, JC (1996) *Spirited Women: Gender, women and cultural identity in the Nepal Himalaya*, Columbia University Press: New York.

Notes

1 People of Dzong
2 People of Barabong
3 Noble households were excluded from the *drongba* system, as it was they in the past who benefited from it.
4 The beliefs of the Baragongba about where the *lu* live and how they must be treated translate into practical rules concerning hygiene and health, as well as rules which protect the environment (Mumford 1989).

Gender relations, 'Hindu' nationalism, and NGO responses in India

Stacey Burlet

This article explores the strategies that non-government organisations (NGOs) are using to challenge the right-wing nationalism presently dominating Indian politics. Development workers must be sensitive to the importance of religion, but also avoid getting caught up in religious conflict. Gender issues, which straddle religious and political boundaries, can end up marginalised.

In India, approximately 30,000 NGOs are providing training and tools to improve people's living conditions, and to build sustainable livelihoods (http://www.anand.to/india/ngo.html). However, their ability to do this is increasingly affected by right-wing nationalist ideologies which dominate national politics, and by escalating levels of violence at local level. There often is a thin line for NGOs between acknowledging the importance of religion in people's lives, and avoiding collusion with political factions which seek power through asserting religious identification above all other criteria. This balancing act has often diminished NGOs' ability to define their own agendas in areas such as gender relations. As a result, women's rights have been marginalised at national level, unless they are directly linked to the status of communities defined in terms of religion.

The Hindu tradition: source of repression and resistance

The concept of patriotism, the requirement that citizens prove their allegiance to the 'nation', and debates on the rightful place of the 'majority', have framed political debates in India since the late 1960s.[1] Nationalist actors have taken this one step further. A variety of organisations which claim that Hindus are 'one people' and 'one nation' linked by blood, belief, and belonging, are working in many sectors such as education to bring this goal to fruition. During research for this article[2], I was told: 'Hindus are not only a community, … they are a nation and Hinduism is a way of life. Hindu unity is a must. In the past we were disunited, in the future we will be united' (interview with the General Secretary of the Vishwa Hindu Parishad, a cultural organisation, 1996).

However, the accuracy of 'Hinduism' as a term which denotes a single religious tradition, based on which people express their political desires, is questionable. According to the 1991 Census of India, 82 per cent of the Indian population are Hindu (http://www.census india.netreligion.html, 1999)[3]. Yet, unlike other religious traditions, Hinduism encompasses a diversity of belief and ritual practice (Oberoi 1994). Originally used to denote the geographical location of a people who lived beyond the river Indus (Sindhu), the term's meaning fundamentally altered during British colonial rule, when it was used to describe all religions evolving from within the Indian subcontinent, including local traditions, as well as Sikhism, Jainism, and Buddhism, despite their distinctive histories, beliefs, and socio-cultural practices (Flood 1996).

This 'catch-all' religious definition also acquired political meaning. The British colonial authorities awarded communities defined in terms of religion a new role in administrative affairs, creating politically ambitious elites who established new alliances with others of the same religion in an attempt to harness power and resources. At the same time, social reformers and political activists such as Gandhi used the term 'Hindu' to describe the common religious beliefs and socio-cultural practices which, in their view, linked the majority of Indians during their struggle for national independence.

This linking of religious identity to political issues led to a hardening of boundaries between groups defined according to religion, particularly between those who were defined as part of the majority – Hindus – and the largest minority grouping – Muslims, who feared that Indian independence would result in their subjugation within a Hindu-dominated state. Polarised demands between those who wanted freedom for all in a united state, and those who wanted freedom and the establishment of a Muslim homeland, led to escalating levels of Hindu-Muslim violence during the latter days of the independence struggle (Oberoi 1994). Although independence was marked by the partition of India and the creation of Pakistan as a Muslim-majority state, India opted for a secular constitution, reflecting its desire to build a nation in which all would be regarded equal, irrespective of their religious, caste, or ethnic identity. Until recently, political parties and the populace largely complied with the commitment to a secular state; political actors who sought to formalise the relationship between Hinduism and the state were consistently marginalised.

Patriot games and party politics: politicising religion?

However, since the mid-1980s, political debates in India have pivoted on identity issues. Right-wingers argue that India can only maintain its territorial integrity and internal cohesion if it establishes a state–society system which reflects the 'national majority's thinking'. This argument is rooted in the belief that successive governments have cynically misused the policy of secularism, in attempts to gather votes and secure power bases among minority groupings. This strategy is believed to have encouraged corruption and violence, and to have plunged Indian society and the economy into deep crisis. For example, the 1998 manifesto of the Bharatiya Janata Party (BJP) states: 'minorities have been cynically used for the purpose of garnering votes these past 50 years, but socio-economic problems have been unattended', and suggests this situation can be remedied by 'energiz[ing] the vision of every patriotic Indian to see our beloved country emerge as a strong, prosperous and confident nation, occupying her rightful place in the international community' (http://www.bjp.org/manifes/manifes.html, 1999).

Organisations using such arguments often simultaneously employ exclusive or inflammatory statements. For example, some minority groups, especially Muslims, are cast as impeding 'national development' through their demands for 'special' rights, and because their religious affiliations extend beyond India's boundaries (Graham 1990). This fractured political climate has also been characterised by growing Hindu–Muslim violence: while before the 1980s, incidents had primarily occurred in 'sensitive' urban areas, previously 'safe' areas have been increasingly affected (Fox 1990). Similarly, analysis of the 1992-93 Bombay 'riots' indicates that Hindu–Muslim violence is also occurring in middle class areas (Kishwar 1993), and commentators stress that Muslims are being killed in disproportionate numbers during such incidents (Fox 1990).

Key reasons for this growth have been attributed to, first, politicians being more open about their use of extra-constitutional tactics, such as paying criminals to initiate a riot with the aim of securing votes (Kishwar 1993). Second, law and order mechanisms seeming increasingly unwilling or incapable of dealing with those who participate in violence. Official sources acknowledge that the police often participate in or openly condone the use of violence against Muslim, and non- and 'low' caste groupings (Tambiah 1990). In the light of these factors, a view widely expressed throughout India is that the current violence against minority groups is politically motivated, rather than the result of Hindus and Muslims being drawn into an inevitable cycle of conflict (see, for example, Anklesaria and Swaminathan 1990).

This argument seems to have validity as, during the 1980s and early 1990s, a coalition of Muslims and 'low' and non-caste Hindus launched a political challenge in the national arena. Their campaign promised the allevi- ation of inequality, and emphasised the disproportionate social disadvantage which many groups face in comparison to high-caste Hindus. Such an alliance has highlighted the faultlines of the nationalist ideology of a unified Hindus community, and stressed the common socio-economic challenges which cross religious boundaries.[4]

The impact on women

Indian women of all social strata have been affected by the nationalist ideology which permeates political debates and by esca- lating levels of Hindu–Muslim violence. Nationalists have developed effective stra- tegies for 'tapping' women as an electoral resource. These include holding women's prayer meetings, celebrating religious imagery in which female power is celebrated as the source of India's greatness, and promoting female politicians (see Llewellyn 1998).

The attraction of such strategies is reinforced by policies which simultaneously acknowledge the importance of the Hindu religious tradition and make commitments to women's socio-economic upliftment (http:// www.bjp.org/manifes/manifes.html, 1999). However, it is also clear that women's rights have been increasingly interpreted and understood within a framework in which religious identification, and the 'proper' place of the 'national majority' and minority groups in Indian society, take prevalence over gender identity. This means that women's dis- advantages and problems as a social group are neglected, unless an issue directly linked to religious identity emerges. Usually, these cases are controversial, and involve nationalists depicting women as potential victims of Muslim men who are represented as engaging in polygamous, callous, and barbaric behaviour (Kapur and Cossman 1996). For example, one leaflet recently disseminated by the nationalist VHP-Bajarang Dal Sanjeli in Gujarat stated: 'What attitude do Muslim loafers adopt towards *adivasi* women going to fill the river with mud ? How do these loafers entrap helpless *adivasi* women and elderly in the name of helping them ? ... Let us save our sisters and daughters being sold to Arabs from the claws of these people' (quoted in CPI(ML)- New Democracy, 1998).

NGOs, Hindu–Muslim cooperation, and local autonomy

NGOs opposed to the current political climate have evolved a variety of strategies, depend- ing on their links with Northern NGOs or international organisations such as the UN, and on their reliance on foreign funding[5].

Organisations which have links with the international NGO community primarily express their opposition to the current political climate through consciousness- raising and networking strategies. In January 1993, for example, groups working in the area of 'development' came together to pledge their solidarity and support for each other, to exchange their experiences of working in a hostile political climate and to formulate a long-term plan of action for securing true secularism in India (VANI News, 1993). Motivated by the belief that religion should have no role in public affairs, networks have thus been established to lobby state institutions to conduct themselves in accordance with constitutional norms.

In contrast, networks such as the National Alliance of People's Movements (NAPM), which primarily represent community-based organisations (CBOs), oppose the BJP's modernising programme. This is couched in the language of *swadeshi* ('India first') and protectionism, but it also makes clear commitments to liberalisation, integrating India into the world economy, achieving an annual GDP growth rate of 8-9 per cent, and rationalising the public sector (http://www.bjp.org/manifes/manifes.htm, 1999). CBO networks argue that this programme will contribute to the breakdown of communication and socio-economic ties between Hindus and Muslims at local level. They thus aim to promote cooperation between communities defined in terms of religion, through devolving government power: local people's joint decision-making can ensure appropriate socio-economic development and maintain productive local relationships.

Because NGOs' activities at national level have the potential to attract the attention and anger of nationalist actors (see *India Today*, 1993), many choose to operate at a local level for fear of harassment (personal interviews, 1996). Some get involved in initiatives such as direct-action campaigns which spring up when violence breaks out in a locality, or immediately afterwards. For example, street-theatre groups perform 'anti-communalism' plays which show how religion is used to sever local ties and secure political power. Often, the drama exposes the role of politicians and community 'representatives' in organising violence. One play, performed by Nishant Natya Manch, depicts how violence is incited and inflamed for specific ends: a mercenary is paid to throw bags of beef and pork into a temple and a mosque; religious leaders use the language of 'religion in danger' to trigger riots; and tension only

abates when it is discovered that the bags contained human flesh (Mullick 1987).

However, for many people, participation in direct action is an unlikely or an impossible option. Personal opinions and religious beliefs can take second place to the need to survive; many women and men who do not support nationalist ideology cannot afford the time or the potential trouble which opposition might attract. In the early 1990s, subsistence workers in Hyderabad and Bombay were frequently unable to work during the curfews imposed on localities experiencing violence. As a result, many faced starvation and had to borrow money or appeal for patronage to buy food and replace stolen items. Their subsequent economic dependence made it hard for them to involve themselves in activities which potentially challenged the money-lenders and local politicians on whom they relied (Bharatiya Janwadi Aghadi 1993).

Tackling this powerlessness, brought about by impoverishment and economic dependency, is therefore prioritised by those NGOs with appropriate sources of funding. A typical strategy is to set up cooperatives and cross-community initiatives to encourage as well as build on historic relationships of socio-economic and political interdependence between Hindus and Muslims. By emphasising economic interdependence, these strategies seek to strengthen people's awareness of the distinction between personal spiritual beliefs and the true character of India's composite culture, and of the religious rhetoric being disseminated by nationalists for the purpose of securing political power.

However, these approaches have limitations. For example, efforts are frequently concentrated in extremely impoverished communities. This often inadvertently reinforces arguments that poor people indulge in violence because their lack of education makes them excitable, and that this is the fault of successive governments which have failed to implement the majority's will, resulting in under-development and a lack of national integration. For example, Muslims are frequently depicted as educationally 'backward' and thus responsible for communal riots: 'Muslims have been slower to take up on education … [They] are aggressive and believe anything that the mullahs tell them. Recently the mullah said you should not have television sets in your house, and 95 per cent came home and threw out their television sets. Whatever you tell them, they will do. They do not think, they follow' (personal interview, 1996). Because such views are widely held, nationalists have been able to suggest that NGO strategies are an irrelevant response to the overall need for 'national development'.

The importance of NGOs' work has been challenged further by nationalists, who portray them as corrupt and elitist, and rooted in Western thought. Here, nationalists are primarily referring to branches of Northern NGOs, but also to 'indigenous' NGOs which are seen to represent non-Indian views. Often, such arguments are supported by CBOs. A Gandhian activist stated: 'We must stand up to the secular class who are enslaved to secularism, a secularism that is wrong, impedes national integration and the development of India as a nation … They are a class that act like third party intervenors, with their own agendas, who will not allow us [Hindus and Muslims] to sort our relationship out. They have taken over the place of the Britishers … We should … start again from our own civilisation' (personal interview, 1996). Given that some NGOs rely on foreign funds and others are part of global networks, this type of accusation is difficult to challenge. As a result, the activities of those NGOs which have global links tend to be primarily recognised in the communities in which they work; their alternative visions of Indian culture remain at the periphery of national debates.

NGOs, nationalism, and gender issues

A further limitation of the strategies pursued by NGOs with international links relates to the fact that initiatives promoting cooperation between Hindus and Muslims often lack awareness of the specific repercussions which nationalist ideology and Hindu–Muslim violence have in women's lives (Hasan 1994).

My own research indicated that many organisations work mainly with men because they are seen as most likely to participate in violence; others view women's oppression as a secondary issue compared with the need to counteract the nationalist agenda. Other reasons given by NGOs for their unwillingness to tackle the gender dimensions of nationalism include the belief that they already risk attracting the hostility of people and groups with vested interests. They argue that incorporating consciousness-raising elements into their work which draw attention to the way in which women are targeted by nationalist actors in their initiatives, might invoke male resistance and limit the credibility of their demands to challenge nationalist ideology. These NGOs advocate that initiatives aiming to empower women should remain separate, and concentrate on alleviating their socio-economic deprivation through the promotion of micro-credit schemes, education, and health-care services (personal interviews, 1996). NGOs thus often purposely marginalise gender issues, and the particular restraints which women face as a result of Hindu–Muslim conflict remain untackled.

Women's resistance to nationalist ideology

A portrayal of the Hindu community as forward-looking, and the Muslim community as backward-looking, has gained credence in the current political climate. As a result, women's ability to challenge issues of common oppression by working together has been limited (Saghal 1992). This is partly because women's knowledge that they share many problems in their daily lives has decreased, and partly because control over their activities has intensified as a result of escalating levels of violence, which have fostered suspicion about those who belong to 'other' communities, and which have made it physically difficult for women to work together in some areas (Chhachhi 1991). It is also because the Indian women's movement has often made its demands for gender equality on the basis of universal definitions of women. In the current political climate, this has invoked criticism from Muslim women, who argue that this indicates a lack of cultural sensitivity at best and prejudice at worst, because it compromises their religious identity (Kapur and Cossman 1996).

Some feminist activists have taken note of these criticisms, and have altered their strategies to ensure that participants in their organisations can simultaneously assert themselves as women and as members of communities defined in terms of religion. To do this, they have concentrated on criticising the portrayal of majority–minority relations as conflictual. In addition, programmes have been set up to establish contacts with women across the country, especially with those affected by violence, and to form support networks for women's groups working to achieve reform on sensitive issues from within their own communities. Contemporary campaigns have been confined to issues which focus on the socio-economic realities of women's lives (Butalia 1996).

Despite these problems, and the marginalisation of women's rights issues by many NGOs, women have devised their own resistance strategies. For example, during incidents of Hindu–Muslim violence, women often intervene to protect and save people from other communities (Confederation of Voluntary Associations 1995). Many also use their power within their neighbourhood to counteract stereotypes and positively influence reactions towards the 'other' community (personal interviews, 1996). In addition, women often lobby their husbands or sons to set up meetings so that discussions take place on how nationalist activity and violence can be prevented from infiltrating their area. The priest of a temple dedicated to Lord Krishna in Maharashtra described how violence was prevented in his area: 'We

[Krishna devotees and Muslims] share a wall. There is a tree where flowers are grown in the mosque complex, which we use for worship [in the temple]: every day the Muslims gather the flowers and give them to us. Around us, half are Hindu, half Muslim, and we have not fought. Women talked. We talked. We decided we wanted peace and to live together … We have let no outside influences disturb this peace. Political parties have not got anywhere in this town because we have decided that we will live by this decision' (personal interview, 1996).

Women's motivations for such activities are often based on the belief that although there are differences between Hindus and Muslims, this should not justify unequal treatment or be the measure by which justice is meted out. As one woman told me, 'for me, my religion, your religion, everybody's religion is sacred, there is no difference – we are all humans, rich or poor, brother or sister, Muslim, Christian, Sikh, Jain, Parsi – all the same. But for politicians and bad people, they use these things to divide us. They pick on something sore and go away when people fight' (personal interview, 1996).

Women also justify their resistance on the basis of socio-economic arguments. For example, in 1993, a number of slum-dwelling communities in Bombay formed self-defence militias to protect local Hindus and Muslims from the effects of nationalist activity in their area at the behest of older women (Bharatiya Janwadi Aghadi 1993). They legitimised the action was by arguing that nationalist actors were promoting divisiveness and encouraging violence in trying to secure political power for themselves and their allies. As local people considered their religious and socio-cultural traditions to be as much based on community involvement and cooperation as on distinctive religious beliefs, this political strategy was interpreted as disrespectful and unjust.

Examples such as these indicate that although the dominance of nationalism in India's national political arena is affecting attitudes at regional and local level, people are employing resistance strategies to maintain political and social autonomy. NGOs working in such situations need to be better informed about these strategies, and the role which women play in them. Moreover, they must develop an awareness of the specific problems which women face as a result of nationalist ideology targeting their activities. Not to do so constitutes collusion in the destabilisation of women's previously won citizenship rights, and the privileging of religious affiliations over other aspects of women's and men's identity.

Stacey Burlet is a lecturer in South Asian Area Studies at the University of Bradford, UK. Her address is Department of Social and Economic Studies, University of Bradford, Bradford, West Yorkshire, UK, BD7 1DP. E-mail sdburlet@ bradford.ac.uk

References

Anklesaria, A and Swaminathan, S, 'Tackling Toyota Hinduism: Restore The State's Moral Authority', *Times of India*, 5 October 1990.

Bharatiya Janwadi Aghadi (1993) *India's Saffron Surge: Renaissance or Fascism?*, Bharatiya Janwadi Aghadi: Bombay.

Butalia, U, 'Mother India', *The New Internationalist* No. 227, March 1996.

Chhachhi, A (1991) 'Forced Identities: the State, Communalism, Fundamentalism and Women in India' in Kandiyoti, D (ed.) *Women, Islam and the State*, Macmillan: London.

Confederation of Voluntary Association and Deccan Development Society (1995) 'Activities Report 1990-95 and Proposed Programme for 1996', COVA and DDS: Hyderabad.

CPI(ML)-New Democracy (1998) 'Gujarat: Minorities in the Storm of Communal Attacks', New Delhi.

Flood, G (1996) *An Introduction to Hinduism*, Cambridge University Press.

Fox, R (1990) 'Hindu nationalism in the making, or the rise of the Hindian' in Fox, R (ed.) *Nationalist ideologies and the production of national cultures*. American Ethnological Society Monograph 2: Chicago.

Graham, B (1990) *Hindu Nationalism and Indian Politics: The Origins and Development of the Bharatiya Janata Sangh*, Cambridge University Press.

Hasan, Z (1994) 'Introduction: Contextualising Gender and Identity in Contemporary India' in *Forging Identities: Gender, Communities and the State in India*, Westview Press: Colorado.

http://www.anand.to/india/ngo.html, 1998

http://www.bjp.org/manifes/manifes.html

http://www.censusindia.net/religion.html, 1999

http://www.censusindia.net/scst.html, 1999

India Today, 'Psychological Warfare', 15 September 1993.

Kapur, R and Cossman, B (1996) *Subversive Sites: Feminist Engagements with Law in India*, Sage Publications: New Delhi.

Kishwar, M, 'Criminalisation of Politics', *Manushi* No. 79, November–December 1993.

'Safety is Indivisible: The Warning from Bombay Riots', *Manushi* No. 74-75, January-February 1993.

Kohli, A (1988) 'Conclusion: State-Society Relations in India's Changing Democracy' in Kohli, A (ed.) *India's Democracy: An Analysis of Changing State-Society Relations*, Princeton University Press.

Llewellyn, J (1998) *The Legacy of Women's Uplift in India*, Sage Publications: New Delhi and London.

Mullick, M,'They're cornering communalism', *The Times of India*, 21 February 1987.

Oberoi, H (1994) *The Construction of Religious Boundaries: Culture, Identity, and Diversity in the Sikh Tradition*, University of Chicago Press.

Saghal, G (1992) 'Secular Spaces: The Experience of Asian Women Organising' in Saghal, G and Yuval-Davis, N (eds.) *Refusing Holy Orders*, Virago Press: London.

Searle-Chatterjee, M (1994) 'Caste, religion and other identities' in Searle-Chatterjee, M and Sharma, U (eds.) *Contextualising Caste: Post-Dumontian Approaches*, Blackwell Publishers: Oxford.

Tambiah, SJ (1990) 'Reflections on Communal Violence in South Asia', *Journal of Asian Studies*, Vol. 49, No. 4.

VANI News, 'Some Suggestions for the Immediate Situation', January 1993.

Notes

1 Since the late 1960s, a crisis of government has been growing since the realisation that the goal of creating a state with opportunity for all remained unfulfilled. This led the Congress Party, which had ruled India for the most part since 1947, to increasingly devise and rely on nationalist and populist arguments to maintain their power. When these strategies failed, and it lost its dominance over the national political arena, a framework had been established in which it was acceptable to discuss the possibility of 'majority' rule and the future direction of the Indian state.

2 The data on which this article draws was collected over a two-year period during which personal interviews were conducted and oral histories collected from NGO and community-based organisation (CBO) activists, politicians and government representatives, social and religious leaders, and people living in rural and urban areas of India.

3 This figure excludes data from the region of Jammu and Kashmir.

4 Clear socio-economic divisions continue to exist among Hindus. These primarily relate to caste, which, from birth, determines a person's status within a hierarchical system, and their duties towards others, depending on his or her gender and stage of life. Caste is determined by a person's *jati* (occupational specialisation) and their *varna* (whether or not they belong to one of the four main categories which make up the caste system). These categories are Brahmans (priests), Kshatriyas (warriors and rulers), Vaisyas (artisans), and Sudras (servants). Traditionally, those ranked lower down in the system were seen to pollute the ritual purity of those higher up. As a result, practical measures developed to ensure that 'high' castes remained uncontaminated by 'lower' castes. The impact of these measures has been especially harsh for peoples alternatively referred to as 'untouchables', *harijans* (Children of God), or 'scheduled castes', which make up 16.48 per cent of the population (1991 Census of India). Some among this group have increasingly criticised high-caste Hindus, arguing that they have no right to represent 'low' and non-caste peoples as part of the same social grouping if they continue to treat them as 'different' and marginalised from India's cultural and social life (Searle-Chatterjee 1994). They have also organised politically in an attempt to secure socio-economic equality, and to voice their opposition to atrocities which continue to be perpetrated against them by high castes in both rural and urban areas (Kohli 1988).

5 It has been estimated that only 41 per cent of the NGOs currently operating in India are registered with the Ministry of Home Affairs under the Foreign Contribution (Regulation) Act, while a further 3 per cent are officially recognised as receiving government funds or foreign donations (http://www.anand.to/india/ngo.html). The remainder are CBOs, operating at a grassroots level.

Religion, male violence, and the control of women:

Pakistani Muslim men in Bradford, UK[1]

Marie Macey

This article examines Pakistani Muslim male violence in the public and private spheres in Bradford, UK, and explores the relationship between this and ideas of culture and religion. It contrasts male and female attitudes to Islam: some men are using it to justify violence against women, while women of all ages and backgrounds are using it in a very different way, as a source of strength and to negotiate (with ingenuity and humour) the cultural and religious requirements which men try to impose on them.

Introduction

'My message is to everyone, the community and the service providers. The needs of Asian women must be recognised and accepted and they should be supported so that they do not return to the vulnerable and dangerous situation that they were originally escaping from. Service providers must take responsibility for addressing the issues and putting the needs of individual Asian women before the needs of the community' (Keighley Domestic Violence Forum (KDVF), 1998).

The above statement was made by a Pakistani woman survivor of male violence at a conference, Domestic Violence in Asian Communities, held in Bradford in 1997. The conference enabled Asian women to express their anger at the general failure of social service providers to acknowledge gender differences in working with Asian communities. Academics, community workers, doctors, lawyers, nurses, the police, politicians, policy-makers, social workers, and teachers were indicted for prioritising 'anti-racist' or 'ethnically sensitive' policy and practice over women's needs. In so doing, they were accused of colluding in women's oppression, as manifested in mental breakdown, depression and suicide as well as disappearances and murders: ' ... there are many cases of daughters, wives or sisters being beaten to death, burned or grievously harmed by their kin ... ' (Afshar 1994, 133).

Bradford, located in the North of England, is the fourth largest urban area in England. Its population is young – 23.6 per cent are under 16 years old – and growing; it is set to increase by 6 per cent by the year 2011. The largest minority ethnic group, of Pakistani origin, is projected to increase by 57.7 per cent between 1998 and 2011 (City of Bradford Metropolitan District Council (BMC) 1998). One in five people in Bradford lives in an area of multiple deprivation characterised by poverty, unemployment, poor education, over-crowded housing, crime, drug dealing, the presence of firearms, and prostitution (BMC 1993 and 1998). Unemployment, currently at 6.4 per cent, is particularly concentrated in the inner city among young people of Pakistani and Bangladeshi origin (BMC 1996a and b). The violence discussed in this article takes place in such socioeconomically deprived 'Muslim residential zones' (Lewis 1994), where people of Pakistani origin are in the overwhelming majority (Ballard 1994). Ethnicity and religion acquire an independent status, both because the perpetrators of violence explicitly use both to justify their actions, and because comparable white areas are not marked by similar levels or types of violence.

The men referred to in this article constitute only a tiny percentage of the local Pakistani Muslim community. The vast majority remains, as they have always been, strictly law-abiding in public and non-violent in private. However, the violence described is of sufficient magnitude to constitute a serious problem to all residents of the city. The young age of the perpetrators and the fact that increasingly, drugs are involved, give further cause for concern (Khan 1997).

Writing on sensitive topics

I acknowledge that some may question the legitimacy of a white, Western woman writing about Pakistani Muslim men's violence in Bradford. Cultural relativists might suggest that the practices of a minority ethnic group cannot be criticised by anyone outside that group. Anti-racists might argue that my writing deflects attention from the oppression of racism, and perpetuates stereotypes. While I acknowledge such dangers, I am unwilling to accept the male domination of the discourse on culture, religion, and violence which renders women's needs – and their suffering – invisible. Women from minority ethnic groups are seeking alliances with women from other groups; I find myself unable, as either social scientist or woman, to ignore their pleas for help. As a social scientist, I agree with Haleh Afshar that a climate of fear and oppression has been created in this area which extends to research and scholarly pursuits (Afshar 1994, 144). This has far-reaching implications for the adequacy of academic analysis, social policy, and practice. As a woman, I am motivated by two memories. At a meeting of the orga-

nisation Women Against Fundamentalism, a young Pakistani woman asked the non-Pakistani women present: 'Where were you when I was being harangued and threatened [by extremist Islamic men]; why weren't you standing beside me?' The second memory, more vivid still, is of the misery in the eyes of another young woman, who told me that she was seriously considering suicide because of her mother's determination to force her into an 'arranged' marriage.[2] She related that nearly every night a man came to the house to 'inspect' her: 'I feel like I'm in a cattle market; they look me up and down and undress me with their eyes; I feel like a whore.'[3]

The research and methodology

The material used in this article was collected over a four-year period from students and staff in further and higher education institutions; from working women (prostitutes); from survivors of domestic violence; from police personnel who work with Asian women fleeing domestic violence or forced arranged marriages; from the staff of a drugs project for young Asian men; from the staff of an agency for Asian women who suffered domestic violence; and from staff of a children's society working with teenage prostitutes. Methods included participant and non-participant observation at meetings, conferences, Islamic society events, lectures, seminars, focus groups, and interviews. Much key information was gathered through conversations which enabled speakers to discuss sensitive and sometimes painful issues and experiences.

Data from small-scale empirical research conducted by students of Pakistani origin has also been used. Like my research, this was conducted in such diverse settings as informants' homes, schools, domestic violence units, psychiatric hospitals and day centres, maternity hospitals, drug abuse centres, and on street corners. One of the most striking aspects of the research is the high level of congruence between accounts produced by very disparate informants; so material which may at first sight appear impressionistic is in fact grounded in the lived reality of Bradford people, particularly Pakistani women.[4]

Pakistani Muslim male violence in Bradford[5]

The public sphere

From the 1960s to the present time, there has been a significant shift from orderly public protest to overt violence as a response to the situation of the Pakistani community. In the 1960s and 1970s, Pakistani and white people united in peaceful protest against the growth of right-wing politics in the area and the 'bussing' of immigrant children to schools in the suburbs. In the 1980s, the focus of protest changed to demands for recognition of religious difference (for the provision of *halal* meat in schools, for instance). In 1989, the 'Rushdie Affair'[6] involved a ritual public burning of Salman Rushdie's novel, *The Satanic Verses*, followed by demonstrations which degenerated into public disorder. In 1995, gangs of young Pakistani men roamed the streets during the local elections, harassing political rivals and residents. This was followed by a campaign against the sex trade which started as an organised peaceful protest but degenerated into gangs violently harassing working women (prostitutes). The men succeeded in driving the prostitutes(both black and white, and mostly teenagers) out of the area, demonstrating their ability to organise over a wide geographical area *and* using Islam as a mobilising force. This 'success' may have built on the gang activity during the elections to become a contributory factor in encouraging young Muslim men subsequently to engage in the public disorder known as the Bradford Riots (see note 5).

Today, violence in the public sphere in Bradford is perpetrated by gangs of Pakistani youths and directed at all sectors of the population. However, a favourite target is young Asian women, many of whom now refuse to walk in certain areas. This supports Hanmer's argument that it is not only actual violence, but *fear* of violence which constrains and controls women's behaviour (1978). One young woman gave up her full-time degree course because she could not cope with the daily harassment by gangs of about a dozen youths. They prevented her reaching her car, jumping on it, and calling her names such as 'slut' and 'slag'. Her parents were telephoned and harangued as 'bad parents' and 'a disgrace to the community'.

The private sphere

The existence of male violence against women[7] in the Pakistani community in Bradford is not surprising, since domestic violence transcends all social divisions (Hanmer 1978; Hanmer and Saunders 1993); however, it has been denied by religious leaders and other male members of the community.[8] Nor is it surprising that traditionally closed communities which feel under siege from racism and anti-Islamic sentiment from outside (Khanum 1992) should seek to preserve an image of themselves as harmonious. However, what is shocking to women in and outside the community is the collusion of religious leaders and employees of racial equality organisations in the situation. Survivors of domestic violence have reported that the former tell them to go home and behave as dutiful wives, and the latter state that interference in domestic issues is outside their remit (KDVF 1998).

Crossing the public–private divide

Violence which crosses the public–private divide is organised and structured through Pakistani male networks (termed 'the mobile phone mob' by Asian women). This is targeted at Pakistani people, centres around *izzat* (family and community honour),[9] and involves assertions of misdemeanour or offence on religious grounds. The tactics deployed include threatening young women's parents in anonymous telephone calls; putting aggressive pressure on young women to stay at home; organising searches for women who have fled home and issuing death threats to gays and lesbians; and circulating leaflets exhorting Muslim men to rape Sikh women and murder homosexuals[10]. One young woman said that she cannot go out in Bradford to socialise because: 'the harassment got too much for my parents and my dad eventually asked me to go outside Bradford for nights out because he couldn't take any more'. Others explain male pressure on women to stay in the home as rational self-interest. One explained, 'we'd see what they're up to – and what they're up to is adultery, having fun and making money from drugs and prostitution. Obviously, they wouldn't want their wives to know what's going on, would they?' (personal conversations).

Society, culture, and religion

Religion can be used by individuals, groups, and societies in a variety of ways; it can serve to oppress or liberate, to comfort or kill. It is an extremely powerful resource which has been intimately involved in the construction of our world (Allen and Macey 1995). In the UK today – partly as a result of the links between modernity and secularisation – religion tends to be regarded by the state and other institutions as a personal matter. However, this ignores the reality of multi-cultural societies containing minority ethnic groups to whom religion is a central element of identity (Yinger 1986; Rex 1991). It also ignores the reality of Islam as a significant force in the post-modern world (Kepel 1994; Lewis and Schnapper 1994): it is a source of community cohesion, not just of personal strength and hope, to believers (Afshar 1989; Modood 1989; Lutz 1991; Macey 1992).

The form and focus of religion varies and is strongly influenced by its wider social context, so that culture and religion are almost inseparable (Afshar 1989; Allen and Macey 1994). The speed and extent of change is an important influence on religion. Fundamentalism tends to gain popularity in situations of rapid change or conflict, and among people in a state of social transition (Macey 1991; Neilsen 1984; Robinson 1988). Where religion is involved in struggles against inequality and oppression, it tends towards one of two extremes: the highly orthodox (reactionary) or the radical (revolutionary).

Male violence, religion, and the policing of women

All the above factors apply to Pakistani Muslim men in Bradford, and may go some way towards explaining their simultaneously defensive and aggressive behaviour. One aspect of religion which seems almost immune to social change is its disproportionate impact on women relative to men. This is partly a consequence of patriarchy, but also a result of women's central role as transmitters of the faith to subsequent generations. In Pakistani communities in Britain, women are central to cultural, as well as religious, reproduction: they must be guarded as both custodians of the faith and as carriers of responsibility for the very survival of a community which sees itself under threat. When survival is felt to be at issue, violence often follows.

It is not entirely surprising, then, that young men in Bradford police 'their' women so rigorously (Alibhai-Brown 1998). In Pakistani communities throughout Britain, Muslim men display great concern over 'appropriate' female dress and behaviour, because these are taken to signify not only women's honour, but that of their families and of the wider community (Afshar 1994; Kassam 1997). The importance attached to 'appropriate' women's clothing may also symbolise the deeper fear of corruption by the West and the threat to traditional values and morals.[11] Even university students are under constant surveillance as their male peers form 'intelligence networks' to report inappropriate dress, immodest behaviour or unapproved relationships to the community (Ali 1992, 119). The relative freedom of university comes at a price. However, it is a small price compared with that paid by their less privileged peers, including those who are forced to flee family, friends, and community to escape domestic violence, those suffering breakdown, and depression and those who kill themselves. They also include the women who simply vanish, and those on whose suspicious deaths the Coroner's office is unwilling to release information (Alibhai-Brown 1998).

Like religion, violence is also a powerful resource. Ann Campbell (1993) argues that male violence bestows rewards including social control, normative approval, and an established masculine identity. In Bradford, some young Pakistani men have constructed a form of Islamic identity which affords them peer-group status, community approval, *and* control over women. As their female counterparts observe, this enables them 'to have the best of all worlds': 'Western' in their attitudes to clothes, alcohol, drugs, and prostitution; 'Muslim' in dealing with service providers and Pakistani women.

Women's attitudes to religion, peace, and transformation

Women involved in this research were highly critical of men's (ab)use of Islam to justify violence, seeing this as the antithesis of religious and cultural teaching. They themselves use religion in a very different way. For example, women's involvement in the Bradford Riots was restricted to two peacemaking initiatives. Some women organised a petition, signed by 172 women, which stated: 'As women we feel sad about what happened at the weekend. We want everybody to listen to each other. We want peace'. Four Asian and four white women, from the group Interfaith Women for Peace, marched through the disturbances, carrying candles and a banner saying 'Peace' in Arabic, English, and Urdu (Allen and Barrett 1996). Such women, far from being passive victims of community oppression, confirm Alibhai-Brown's observation that: 'acts of defiance … occur daily in the lives of Muslim women in Northern England. Even in the tightest, most vigilant of communities, women make love, or their own form of war, practice "illicit" contraception in a variety of relationships, make unlikely friends, have abortions. At the same time the men proclaim that such things cannot happen in Muslim communities, their own hypocrisies … conveniently forgotten!' (1992, 120).

Young women, particularly those educated in Britain, are able to use both religion and culture to challenge patriarchal norms and achieve their own goals. One young woman recounted how she had demanded access to university as a right enshrined in Islamic teaching, supporting her statements with Qu'ranic references: 'It took me two years, but in the end they [parents] gave in. I think it was mainly to shut me up!' Another postponed an unwanted marriage *and* gained additional education by manipulating Pakistani culture: 'I just kept telling my parents how much more I'd be worth in the marriage market with a Master's degree'. A third woman used British culture to defer an arranged marriage: 'I've just used what I learned on the [assertiveness training] course to handle my Dad. We used to have screaming rows every night; now I just say to him 'I hear what you're saying … however … ' and I stay really calm … and he can't hack it, he just doesn't know what to do'. These women are constructively combining arguments derived from cultural and religious practice to achieve some degree of autonomy in a potentially highly restrictive situation.

Conclusion

Notwithstanding the above examples of gains by, and for, Muslim women, many pressures are put on them by both the Pakistani and white communities. Instances of the former may stem from culture, religion, patriarchy, or any combination of the three. They include coercion to marry kin from Mirpur; domestic violence; increasing vigilance in policing (and young men's demonstrated ability to track down offenders via networks across the UK). Examples of pressures rooted in white society stem largely from the complex interaction of sexism and racism, as well as a genuine desire not to offend. Whatever the motivation, this leads to essentialising minority ethnic communities and perhaps prioritising 'anti-racist' or 'ethnically sensitive' perspectives. The outcome is gender-blind policy and practice which operate to disadvantage women.

For example, when women seek police protection against forced marriages, there is a stark choice between responding *either* to men's demands for the return of 'their' women *or* to women's demands for refuge. The two are not reconcilable. This seems self-evident in relation to white people, but racism (sometimes in the guise of anti-racism or respect for cultural differences) leads to the treatment of black and Asian communities as undifferentiated entities unmarked by social divisions such as class and gender. This approach may satisfy political and pragmatic expediency, but it constitutes a denial of women's human rights. Pragna Patel blames the dominance of multi-cultural ideology for the widespread failure to cut through community obstacles to address the needs of Asian women. Her message needs to be heard – and acted on – by development workers, service providers, social scientists, and policy-makers:

' … what multi-culturalism does (in return for information and votes) is to concede some measure of autonomy to community leaders to govern their communities. In reality this means that community leaders have most control over the family, women and children. Together with the state, community leaders define the needs of the minority communities then limit and separate progressive voices on the grounds of these being inauthentic and westernised. More radical elements of our community are labelled as extremists. This is the result of multi-cultural policies. They have had an enormous and devastating impact on women's autonomy and rights … ' (1998, 22).

Marie Macey is a senior lecturer in Sociology in the Department of Applied Social Studies, University of Bradford, BD7 1DP. Fax: +44 (1274) 235 690. E-mail: m.macey@bradford.ac.uk

References

Afshar, H (1989b) 'Women and reproduction in Iran' in Anthias, F and Yuval-Davis, N (eds.) *Woman - Nation - State*, Macmillan: London.

Afshar, H (1989a) 'Gender Roles and the "Moral Economy of Kin" among Pakistani Women in West Yorkshire' in *New Community*, Vol. 15, No. 2.

Afshar, H (1994) 'Muslim Women in West Yorkshire: Growing up with Real and Imaginary Values amidst Conflicting Views of Self and Society', Afshar, H and Maynard, M (eds.) *The Dynamics of 'Race' and Gender: Some Feminist Interventions*, Taylor and Francis: London.

Ali, Y (1992) 'Muslim Women and the Politics of Ethnicity and Culture in Northern England' in Sahgal, G and Yuval-Davis, N (eds.) *Refusing Holy Orders: Women and Fundamentalism in Britain*, Virago: London.

Allen, S and Barrett, J (1996) *The Bradford Commission Report*, The Bradford Congress, HMSO: London.

Allen, S and Macey, M (1995) 'Some Issues of Race and Ethnicity in the 'New Europe': Rethinking Sociological Paradigms' in Brown, P and Crompton, R (eds.) *The New Europe: Economic Restructuring and Social Exclusion*, UCL. Press Ltd: London.

Alibhai-Brown (1998) 'God's Own Vigilantes', *The Independent*, 12 October 1998.

Ballard, R (1994) 'The Emergence of Desh Pardesh' in Ballard, R (ed.) *Desh Pardesh: The South Asian Presence in Britain*, C. Hurst and Co.: London.

Campbell, A (1993) *Out of Control: Men, Women and Aggression*, London: Pandora

Choudry, S (1996) *Pakistani Women's Experience of Domestic Violence in Great Britain*, Research Findings No. 43, Home Office Research and Statistics Directorate: London.

City of Bradford Metropolitan District Council (1993) *Areas of stress within Bradford District*, Research Section: Bradford.

City of Bradford Metropolitan District Council (1996a) *Bradford and District Economic Profile,*, Economic Information Service: Bradford.

City of Bradford Metropolitan District Council (1996b) *Bradford and District Demographic Profile*, Educational Policy and Information Unit: Bradford.

City of Bradford Metropolitan District Council (1998) *Bradford and District Economic Profile, July Update*, Economic Information Service: Bradford.

Hanmer, J (1978) 'Violence and the Social Control of Women' in Littlejohn, G et al. (eds.) *Power and the State*, Croom Helm: London.

Hanmer, J with Saunders, S (1993) *Women, Violence and Crime Prevention: A Community Study in West Yorkshire*, Gower: London.

Khan, A (1997) 'An Examination of Drug Use Within the 'Pakistani' Community in Bradford' unpublished BA dissertation.

Khanum, S (1992) 'Education and the Muslim Girl', G. Sahgal and N. Yuval-Davis (eds.) in *Refusing Holy Orders: Women and Fundamentalism in Britain*, Virago: London.

Keighley Domestic Violence Forum (1998) Conference on Domestic Violence in Asian Communities, KDVF/University of Bradford.

Kepel, G (1994) *The Revenge of God: The Resurgence of Islam, Christianity and Judaism in the Modern World*, Polity Press: London.

Lewis, P (1994) *Islamic Britain*, London: I.B. Tauris.

Lewis, B and Schnapper, D (eds.) (1994) *Muslims in Europe*, London: Pinter Publishers.

Lutz, H (1991) 'The Myth of the 'Other': Western Representation and Images of Migrant Women of so-called Islamic Background' in *International Review of Sociology*, 2.

Macey, M (1991) 'Christian Fundamentalism: The Growth of a Monster?', paper presented to the Women in Society Seminar Series, University of Bradford.

Macey, M (1992) 'Greater Europe: Integration or Ethnic Exclusion?' in *The Political Quarterly*, 63:5.

Macey, M (1995) 'Towards Racial Justice? A Re-evaluation of Anti-Racism' in *Critical Social Policy*, Vol.15:2/3, Autumn 1995.

Macey, M and Moxon, E (1996) 'An Examination of Anti-Racist and Anti-Oppressive Theory and Practice in Social Work Education' in *British Journal of Social Work*, 26.

Modood, T (1989) 'Religious Anger and Minority Rights' in *The Political Quarterly*, Vol. 60 (3).

Neilsen, JS (1984) *Muslim Immigration and Settlement in Britain*, Centre for the Study of Islam and Christian-Muslim Relations: Birmingham.

Patel, P (1998) Southall Black Sisters', keynote address to the Conference on Domestic Violence in Asian Communities, KDVF/University of Bradford.

Rex, J (1991) *Ethnic Identity and Ethnic Mobilisation in Britain*, Monographs in Ethnic Relations No. 5, ESRC/Centre for Research in Ethnic Relations: Warwick.

Robinson, F (1988) *Varieties of South Asian Islam*, Centre for Research in Ethnic Relations: Warwick.

Rushdie S (1988) *The Satanic Verses*, Viking Books: London.

Sahgal, G and Yuval-Davis, N (eds.) (1992) *Refusing Holy Orders: Women and Fundamentalism in Britain*, Virago: London.

Shaw, A (1994) 'The Pakistani Community in Oxford' in Ballard, R (ed.), *Desh Pardesh: The South Asian Presence in Britain*, C Hurst and Co.: London.

Spadacini, B and Nichols, P (1998) 'Campaigning against female genital mutilation in Ethiopia using popular education' in *Gender and Development*, Vol. 6, No. 2, July 1998.

Yinger JM (1986) 'Intersecting strands in the theorisation of race and ethnic relations' in Rex, J and Mason, D [eds], *Theories of Race and Ethnic Relations*, Cambridge University Press.

Notes

1 The term 'Pakistani' is inaccurate: most of the young men referred to in this article are British and, if not actually born in England, have spent most of their lives here. I retain the term because official documents, statistics, and the men themselves use it. Their origins, in the Mirpur region of Kashmir, remain an important influence, as does Islam (Afshar 1989; Modood 1988). Culture and religion are not easily separable, and much of what is transmitted as religious code is actually cultural tradition.

2 This example illustrates the fact that the distinction between arranged and forced marriages is not always clear-cut. The former are traditional among communities from the Indian sub-continent and are widely accepted by young South Asian women (Afshar 1989). The latter go against Qu'ranic teaching and are said by Choudry (1966) to be rare and decreasing. However, in Bradford young women are put under intense pressure to accept arranged marriages which sometimes take place without any prior meetings between the partners or after only one meeting in the presence of family. The local Area Community Officer (a police-funded post) currently carries a caseload of 750 Asian women fleeing their homes to escape violence or forced marriages (KDVF 1998).

3 For a more detailed discussion of these issues, see Allen and Macey 1995, on social science research; Macey 1995, on anti-racist social policy; Macey and Moxon 1996, on anti-racist social work; and Spadacinni and Nichols 1998, on cultural relativism.

4 It is notable that students of Pakistani origin have considerably more difficulty in obtaining information from Pakistani people than I do. Some reasons for this are touched on in the article, but the fact is revealing of levels of oppression in Bradford. It also has implications for the conventional wisdom on matching ethnicity in research.

5 This section rests heavily on *The Bradford Commission Report*, an inquiry into the public disorders in Bradford in 1995 (Allen and Barratt 1996), when 300 youths burned barricades, looted shops, wrecked cars, fire-bombed businesses and issued death threats at knife point. The Commission's task was to understand why a minor policing incident was followed by two nights of public disorder, involving violence by young Pakistani men against other ethnic groups. To this end, public meetings were held and evidence taken from about 300 people.

6 This refers to demands to ban the sale of Salman Rushdie's novel, *The Satanic Verses*, on the grounds that it was blasphemous. Many Muslim men in Britain engaged in widespread protest, including threats of arson and death against retailers who stocked the book, and public support was proclaimed for the *fatwa* issued against Rushdie by the Ayatollah Khomeni. In contrast, Muslim women, along with other Asian and black women, mainly demonstrated in support of the right to free speech. For a discussion of the longer-term effects of the 'Rushdie Affair' on Muslim women, see Khanum 1992.

7 Women are also implicated in violence against women, as both instigators and perpetrators and, although this is publicly denied, it is testified to by women survivors, workers in domestic violence agencies, social workers, and health visitors (KDV 1998).

8 It is not clear whether domestic violence is increasing or whether it is simply that more women are willing or able to speak out about it than in the past. What is clear is the association between domestic violence and suicide and the fact that Asian women's suicide rate in Britain is three times the national average (Patel 1998).

9 Although *izzat* is central to Islamic culture, the burden of upholding family and community honour rests solely on women (Khanum 1992) and is maintained by 'guarding' women (Afshar 1994).

10 These are traceable to extremist Islamic organisations operating in the UK but funded from overseas (see Rex 1991 for a broader discussion of the resurgence of Islam and its power as a mobilising force).

11 All migrant communities ossify and idolise ideas about their past (Afshar 1994; Shaw 1994) but change occurs over time. The Bradford Pakistani community has taken steps to resist change, including arranged marriages with close kin from Mirpur (around 700 such families are established every year in Bradford) and importing *Imams* who preach a particular version of Islam (Lewis 1994).

A double-edged sword: Challenging women's oppression within Muslim society in Northern Nigeria

Fatima L. Adamu

Islamic development NGOs find it difficult enough to finance their work, because Western donors are often reluctant to sponsor NGOs with religious affiliations. Muslim women activists working to achieve development with gender equity face an even greater challenge: they must secure funding as well as justify their goals to those within their societies who see feminism as a threat.

Until recently, there has been a muted relationship between 'gender and development' and religion, in spite of the importance of religion in the lives of many women who are the beneficiaries of gender and development (GAD) programmes. As a Muslim woman activist involved in work on gender issues in Northern Nigeria, I consider the issue of religion to be particularly relevant to the policy and practice of GAD in Muslim societies. Because gender issues are both religious and political concerns in many Muslim societies (Hale 1997; Mernissi 1996), any attempt to reform gender relations that excludes religion is likely to fail.

Currently, Muslim women in many communities throughout the world are re-defining Islam as a legitimate tool for engaging with and tackling gender issues in Muslim societies (Baden 1992). It is true that interpretations of Islam have been used by leaders in the past, and are still used today, as grounds for refusing women their rights as individuals, including access to secular, 'Western' education and the right to participate equally in politics (Callaway and Creevey 1994). In Nigeria, women's right to be elected to the secular central government is being challenged in the name of Islam. Consequently, Hausa women of Muslim faith in Northern Nigeria are being left far behind, compared with their sisters from the South (ibid.).

Nigeria is a secular state, but the majority of the population in Northern Nigeria are Muslims. The Hausa people are the dominant ethnic group in the region. It is estimated that Hausa is the largest ethnic group in Africa, with a population of 50-60 million (Furniss, 1996). Islam reached Northern Nigeria via trans-Saharan trade routes, about the eleventh and twelfth century. By the nineteenth century, Islam had become part of the cultural identity of the Hausa (Imam, 1991). The impact of Islam on the Hausa people society was deep and widespread, and it is difficult to separate the two cultures: the Jihad movements of the early nineteenth century, which aimed to 'purify' Islam and prevent it mixing with indigenous traditional beliefs, had a far-reaching impact on Northern Nigeria.

Few attempt to underplay the centrality of Islam in determining the position of women in Muslim societies, and its impact on the everyday lives of women. In such societies, ideas about gender relations are derived from interpretations of Islam, and these ideas are enacted either through legislation or public opinion. Matters of central concern to women such as inheritance, marriage, child custody, divorce, and other marital relationships are governed by Islamic rules in many Muslim societies. In Northern Nigeria, the Shari'ah courts, which practise Islamic personal law, remain the most relevant and widely used legal system, despite the option of using the civil court. Legal matters which concern women in their role as wives and mothers – for example, disputes over inheritance, marriage, divorce, and child custody – are therefore commonly conducted or resolved within the Islamic legal system rather than the parallel Nigerian civil legal system.

In questioning such issues, Muslim feminists have found themselves in the middle of a conflict between Islam and the 'West', facing a double-edged sword. The importance and relevance of women's participation in the Islamic movement, and the emergence of Islamic women's movements in the Muslim world, have been interpreted by some as 'an ambiguous political struggle', where women are on the one hand 'fighting actively against their inequality, but on the other [are] accepting or supporting their own sub-ordination' (Duval 1997, 39). But despite conflicting interpretations of our struggle, the fact of the matter is that Muslim women activists are confronting issues of concern to the generality of Muslim women; and we are doing so in our own way. This article is my personal reflection on this struggle. What are the consequences for women who attempt to reform gender relations in Muslim societies? What problems do we encounter, and how do they relate to the ideas, plans, and programmes of GAD?

GAD, Islam, and the West

GAD can be seen as a battlefield in which the conflict between Islam and the West is played out in Muslim societies. While much writing on women and development in Muslim societies from Western academic researchers and media commentators shows a lack of understanding and bias (Callaway and Creevey 1994; Toynbee 1997), GAD is viewed with suspicion by some Muslim scholars as offering a means to the West to wipe out the values and beliefs of Muslim societies. Some Western writers do indeed suggest that Muslim women may be used to attack Islam and undermine Islamic values. Mervyn Hiskett, for example – a British scholar who has spent years in Northern Nigeria and who has written on how to deal with the expansion of Islam in the West – describes women as the 'Islam's Achilles' heel'; his solution is the assimilation of Muslim women into 'Western' culture (Faruqi 1994).

Bugaje, a Nigerian Islamic scholar, who is a liberal on gender issues, echoed these suspicions in his 1997 discussion of women's empowerment: 'these two decades, during which the UN championed the globalisation of women's issues, happened to be the two decades during which the UN became increasingly a tool in the hands of a few Western nations who were using it to achieve their selfish political goals. ... This left many Muslims unsure about the role of the UN in respect of women's issues' (Bugaje 1997, 9). While I would wish to challenge such general suspicions on the part of Muslim scholars, they are borne out to some extent by certain UN documents dealing with women, which emphasise individual rights more than responsibilities and community rights. Moreover, the incompatibility of the documents with some Islamic values – especially regarding inheritance law, moral values and practice, and the role and nature of the family – is apparent. For instance, Article 15.4 of the UN Convention on the Elimination of all Forms of Discrimination Against Women (CEDAW) says: 'States Parties shall accord to men and to women the same rights with regard to the law relating to the movement of persons and the freedom to choose their residence and domicile'. While this may seem reasonable, problems arise in practice for

Muslim women, since it is incompatible with Islamic ideas of household relations, and the division of responsibility between husband and wife. Once a marriage contract is fully concluded and enacted, it is the husband's responsibility to provide the material and sexual needs of his wife. In return, the movements and activities of the wife outside the household need the consent of the husband. In Hausa society, the principle of male responsibility for maintenance is reinforced by the fact that it is seen as socially appropriate for a wife to seek divorce if her husband fails to support her. Records from courts in Sokoto from 1988 to 1998 shows that 53 per cent of the civil cases brought before the court (not all of which are concerned with divorce) are maintenance-related .

Other principles adopted in international documents carry similar messages. In the Forward-Looking Strategies for the Advancement of Women, agreed at the Third World Conference on Women in Nairobi in 1991, the 50th paragraph agrees that women should have equal rights with men in matters of inheritance. This is incompatible with the Islamic law of inheritance, which gives women half of what men inherit due to the laws regarding men's responsibility to maintain women.

Moreover, UN documents do not recognise the abuse of women's economic rights inherent within the current Western development model. They therefore fail as an instrument for Muslim women to use in fighting the mismanagement and exploitation of resources in the developing world, both by the elites within those societies, and those in the West.

The practical implications of ignoring Islam for GAD work

Even if such suspicions are unfounded, and GAD programmes are not in principle intended to undermine Islamic values, the exclusion of religion from development discourse and practice is in itself Western in orientation, and contrary to Islamic principle. Perhaps more importantly, it is unrealistic. The lives of women in many Muslim societies, including those of Northern Nigeria, challenge the idea of considering gender issues separately from religion: Islam is not just a religion to which we claim allegiance, or which we mark through performing rituals. It is a total way of life, and we aspire to conduct our lives according to its teachings. In her study of the influence of Islam and Western education on women in Sokoto, northern Nigeria, Knipp (1987) identifies three categories of women: non-Western-educated women, young women, and professional women. Some of their words are presented here.

A non-Western-educated woman says: 'Islam is a great influence on what I say and do, what my relation is supposed to be with my husband, my family[1] and my children' (ibid., 407). Another woman explains: 'Most things that you do in life are guided by the religion: whatever you do, you do for God's sake. … Islam is my religion … it guides one as to how he's going to lead his life' (ibid., 139-140). A young university student says that '… every single thing, how to enter a toilet, how to stay with others, how to acquire knowledge, everything is in the Qur'an … personally, to me, Qur'an is everything' (ibid., 277). One professional women states: 'Islam is a way of life, not a part of life; whatever I do, I hope it conforms with the religion, so more or less all my behaviour, all my acts, I'm praying they conform with the religion. It is more or less my own way of life' (ibid., 406). It can be seen from these words that any GAD initiative which is based on the idea of a separation between women's religious and gender identities will risk alienating and excluding many Muslim women.

An example from my own experience of an initiative which tried to operate in this way is the Family Economic Advancement Programme (FEAP), part of the Nigerian government's poverty-alleviation programme. Since 1996, the government has designated millions of US dollars to assist women with credit to improve their income-generation activities. In order to receive this credit, people are required to form cooperative societies. By this condition, those Muslim women in the north who practise *purdah* (seclusion) are excluded. In 1998, when I was conducting research in Sokoto state, northern Nigeria, many Muslim women in this situation asked me to assist them in forming cooperative societies, in order to meet the credit requirement. The volume of such requests overwhelmed me; I contacted the relevant authorities about this matter, and they promised to look into the case. We started to discuss the idea of getting around the problem of seclusion by forming a cooperative society within an extended or polygynous household (which is the dominant household form in this area). This idea would depend on whether women wished to work with each other in this way within a household; it would also involve visiting individual households in order to make them aware of the opportunity to gain access to credit, in addition to discussing the usual difficulties and problems that may arise. I left the country to study abroad shortly afterwards, and do not yet know the outcome of the discussion and the authority's final decision. If my research had not coincided with the implementation of FEAP, these women might have been overlooked, as was the case with other women's development programmes.

Many GAD programmes are substantially funded by international funding organisa-tions, the majority of which are from Western societies. For Muslim women activists, who need money to fund our programmes, this presents a challenge: we must strike a balance between meeting the requirements of the funding organisations and carrying out our work, as well as balancing this with the opposition we encounter from some quarters of our societies. This is an enormous and difficult task; at the centre of it is our concern for the condition of the women with whom we are working.

'Partnership', donors, and religious NGOs

My concern as a Muslim gender activist has increased in the course of interaction with some funding organisations. Much has been said about the idea of 'partnership' between donors and local NGOs. Although it is an improvement upon the previous relationship between donors and NGOs, we still need to make progress. The organisations and sectors of work which are successful in attaining funding are still chosen almost exclusively by the donors, who define their areas of interest, while local NGOs struggle to fit in. In desperate need of money, some NGOs re-adjust their areas of interest to accommodate the donors' interest, even if this means their work is less useful in responding to the pressing areas of need in the community.

In the 1980s, my experience was that many funding organisations chose not to work with Islamic women's organisations because of their religious orientation. Although this has changed somewhat, this reluctance still resurfaces regularly when interacting with some of them. For example, in March 1998 I attended a workshop on capacity-building and possible partnerships for northern Nigerian NGOs, as part of a project run by the British government's Department for International Development (DFID).[2] When the NGOs were divided into groups, according to the workshop methodology, a disagreement erupted over a request from some participants that there should be a group of religious NGOs (some of us were representing Islamic and Christian organisa-tions). Those opposed to our being grouped together argued that we had been invited not because of our religious affiliations, but in our capacity as NGOs involved with women's development initiatives. We wanted to know what was wrong with being a religious NGO, and who should define the identity of NGOs – themselves, or funders? Do NGOs with a firm rooting in a religion have to appear to change their identity in order to satisfy the donors?

Even after an area of work is mutually identified by a donor and a local NGO which is based on religion, and after funding is agreed, other problems concerned with the issue of religion may arise in the implementation. For instance, in 1994, the director of a US-based funding organisation visited the state where I worked, in search of NGOs with whom to work. During his visit, he made a presentation to representatives of different NGOs on the areas of work for which funding would be provided. Our NGO looked at the areas and – although we were not comfortable with some components in many of them – in consideration of our local needs, we decided to collaborate with the donor in the area of health-care. One of the uncomfortable aspects of this area was the funder's expectation that we would integrate a family-planning component. Our NGO's stand on the issue has been that family-planning is a private affair, with no imposition from any organisation or authority. We duly expressed our concern to the funders, and a consensus was reached in principle. However, in practice it was a challenge to work with the donor because the project, consisting of all the components that the donor expected to see, and its funding, operated as one system; as one part was affected, so also were the others.

While we were having difficulties in dealing with the funding organisation, we had to face another problem of opposition and resentment from the community in which we were working. In particular, the presence of a vehicle that belonged to an American funding organisation on our organisation's premises was misinterpreted by visitors as an indication that we might be bought or used by the USA against Islam.

Lessons and conclusion

In my experience, few women or men in Muslim communities disagree with the content of GAD programmes which address women's practical needs and interests, or even the reform of gender relations, aiming for a fairer society. However, many question GAD programmes on principle, viewing them as illegitimate because they are 'Western'. In line with this, Muslim women activists, including myself, may be branded Western agents, funded by foreign powers to undermine Islam. As a result of this attitude, and funders' mistrust of organisations which have a religious affiliation, the concerns of Muslim women remain unacknowledged and unaddressed. As it is said, 'when two elephants fight, it is the grass that suffers'.

A weakness of many so-called 'gender and development' programmes is that by targeting women and women's issues only, and by excluding men and other issues of wider social interest from the gender/ development discourse and practice, an impression is created that women are the only sex vulnerable to Western influence. In my experience, this may increase Muslim communities' suspicion about what 'gender issues' mean, and harden their stand against interventions which promote women's interests and needs. Focusing on women's rights is seen as a means of diverting attention from the pressing economic and political problems facing many members of Muslim societies, especially in the South and East. Not only are international economic and political bodies involved in this, but local elites are also implicated. In the name of preserving 'tradition', they use the issue of women the debate about women's rights to legitimise their position, and to divert the attention of ordinary people from the soaring unemployment and political oppression that characterise their lives.

Finally, the difficult and fragile relationship between Islamic women's organisations and international donor organisations, which are predominately from Western societies with a Christian heritage, perpetuates the marginalisation of Muslim women activists in the transformation of their society and religion. Since, as I have discussed, Islam is a religion which embraces all aspects of Muslim women's lives, and shapes their experiences, any GAD initiative that attempts to exclude religious concerns from its planning or implementation is likely to exclude Muslim women, and to record a low level of success in addressing their practical needs and long-term interests.

Fatima L Adamu is a lecturer in Sociology at Usmanu Dan Fodiyo University, Sokoto, Nigeria, currently studying for her PhD at the University of Bradford. She is Secretary of the women's health research network in Nigeria, Sokoto state, and has served on many government committees on family, women, and education. You can contact her at the DPPC, University of Bradford, BD7 1DP, e-mail: fladamu@bradford.ac.uk; or at the Dept. of Sociology, Usmanu Dan Fodiyo University, Sokoto, Nigeria, tel. ++234 (60) 234315, e-mail: fladamu@udusok.edu.ng

References

Baden, S (1992) *The Position of Women In Islamic Countries – Possibilities, Constraints and Strategies for Change* , Briefing on Development and Gender, Report No. 4, prepared for special programme, WID, Netherlands Ministry of Foreign Affairs (DGIS), 1994.

Bugaje, U (1997) 'Women's empowerment and Islam', paper presented at a symposium on Islam and contemporary issues, organised by the Movement for Islamic Culture and Awareness, Nigeria.

Callaway, B and Creevey, L (1994) *The Heritage of Islam, Women, Religion and Politics in West Africa*, Lynne Rienner Publishers: London.

Duval, S (1997) 'New veils and new voices: Islamist women's groups in Egypt' in Ask, K and Tjomsland, M (eds.) *Women and Islamisation – Carving a New Space in Muslim Societies*, Chr. Michelsen Institute report series No. 3.

Faruqi, MH (1994) 'Turning xenophobia into social policy – a review of *Some to Mecca Turn to Pray: Islamic Values in the Modern World* by M. Hiskett (The Claridges Press)' in *Impact International*, Vol 24, No 3.

Hale, S (1997) *Gender Politics in Sudan: Islamism Socialism and the State*, Westview Press: Boulder.

Knipp, M (1987) *Women, Western Education and Change: A Case Study of the Hausa-Fulani of Northern Nigeria*, DPhil Dissertation, North Western University.

Mernissi, Fatimah (1996) *Women's Rebellion and Islamic Memory*, Zed Books: London.

Thiam, A (1991) *Speak Out, Black Sisters: Feminism and Oppression in Black Africa*, translated by Dorothy S Blair, Pluto Press: London.

Toynbee, P (1997) 'In defence of Islamophobia', *The Independent*, 23 October 1998, p. 23.

Notes

1 When a Hausa woman says 'family', she is referring to her parents' family, not her marital family, hence the reference to 'husband and my children' as different to 'my family'.

2 The theme of the workshop was 'Capacity Building for Decentralised Development'. It took place in Kano, 10-12 February 1998.

Gender and development from a Christian perspective:

Experience from World Vision

Linda Tripp

Following the example of Christ, who fed the hungry and clothed the poor, the staff and managers of World Vision attempt to incorporate religious faith into their development work as well as their organisational practice. Linda Tripp argues that a spiritual message, combined with practical support, can be more effective in improving the lives of poor people than purely technical help.

In North America, and (I presume) much of Europe, while many still describe themselves as Christian, the outward expression of faith and the role of spirituality in daily life have become almost non-existent for most people. The role of spirituality and religion is deliberately and vigorously kept separate from the 'real' work of development. However, where faith is an integral part of daily living for women and men in communities, and for many development workers, such a separation is not so easily established or maintained.

Giving biblical evidence of Jesus' positive attitude to women's status and needs is a key strategy in promoting our policy on gender with our own staff, partner organisations and with communities in the countries where we work. I also discuss how World Vision itself has developed its organisational position on these issues.

The organisation

World Vision was founded in the US in 1950 during the Korean War. World Vision's founder, Bob Pierce, witnessed the terrible plight of thousands of children who were orphaned or abandoned. Deeply moved, he wrote in his Bible, 'Let my heart be broken with the things that break the heart of God'. His motivation led to the setting up of the World Vision Child Sponsorship Programme. Expanding from that early work with Korean orphanages, World Vision now works at community level in 100 countries, in partnership with local organisations.

Both the organisation's *core values* and its *mission statement* confirm that World Vision is a Christian organisation (Core Values, 22 September 1989); our work includes 'transformational development[1], emergency relief, and promotion of justice[2], public awareness, and sharing the good news of Jesus Christ' (Mission Statement, 17 September 1992). The policies of World Vision reflect a desire to be Christ-like in the world. In Christ, we have a role model who healed the sick, fed the hungry, clothed the naked, and comforted the outcast, and whose message was about restoring relationships and reconciliation. To protect and preserve this Christian ethos and ensure that our work remains grounded in our faith, prayer, and Bible study and teaching are elements of various meetings and discussions. World Vision staff around the world participate in daily devotions and weekly chapel services.

World Vision is not affiliated with any one denomination or church; it is trans-denominational, with staff representing all Protestant denominations as well as the Roman Catholic and Orthodox Churches. Staff around the world, including leadership, are predominantly nationals,[3] who demonstrate that, whether you are from Africa, Asia, Latin America, Europe, the Middle East, or North America, you need not give up your culture to be a Christian.

However, while Christianity defines our organisation's ethos and values, we believe that Christians cannot exclude the possibility of working with groups of other religious or spiritual beliefs. Our work brings us into contact with every major religion throughout the world, and with hundreds of different cultures. World Vision forges partnerships, as appropriate, with women's groups, community leadership, local government, other religious groups, NGOs, international bodies, and the local church. In addition, in countries where the Christian population is very small and local staff are likely to be non-Christian, it is important that they feel comfortable with the values and practices of the organisation.

Words and deeds: linking Christianity and development

In 1993, the Canadian International Development Agency (CIDA), the government agency which distributes and monitors Canada's overseas development assistance, initiated a dialogue with Canadian Christian NGOs with a view to establishing clearer guidelines for working together. The Christian NGOs welcomed this opportunity, and for the next two years participated in lively debates, presented thoughtful papers and invited field partners to explore together with CIDA the role of spirituality in the development process.

In one particular discussion, I stated that World Vision would not be the evangelists of CIDA's doctrine. When my startled government colleague demanded clarification of my comment, I explained that CIDA wants NGOs to focus only on the physical aspects of development – food, water, health-care, agriculture, and so on. Yet the vast majority of people with whom we work in development regard the spiritual realm as equally relevant to daily life, whether they are Christian, Muslim, Buddhist, Hindu, or Animist. To have a relationship with these people, to respect their culture, their wisdom, and their experience, demanded that we also acknowledge the spiritual dimensions of their lives. To promote a secular approach to life would be an insult to them, and inconsistent with our commitment to holistic development.

In his paper *Rethinking a Christian Response to the Poor*, Jayakumar Christian, a senior member of World Vision India, argues that 'the very nature of poverty demands a spiritual response' (Christian 1995). He sees poverty as the result of broken relationships, a distorted interpretation of history, an inadequate world-view of people, exploitation, of poor people's marred identity, and their entrapment in a web of lies. He says, 'Breaking the poverty cycle – whether economically, socially or spiritually – is a threat to those who benefit by keeping the poor underfoot. Being an active Christian organisation requires that World Vision embraces a wide definition of justice and injustice. This can take the form of spiritual injustice as well as physical' (ibid.).

We argued that, where a strong spiritual belief sustains a practice which is harmful, only a spiritual response is appropriate. For example, in a relatively isolated area of Haiti in the 1970s, World Vision found out why a high number of babies were dying of tetanus shortly after birth. Midwives were applying mud to the cut umbilical cord to prevent evil spirits from entering the new-born. Talk of germs and infection fell on deaf ears: the practice had a spiritual basis, and needed a spiritual response. World Vision staff shared their experience of a loving God who was more powerful than the evil spirits. They explained that the mud was unnecessary, since with proper care and love the baby would be strong; but the decision was left to the women. For many of them, the message of a God of love, not fear, was a liberating one, and they decided to stop the practice.

In a bold move, CIDA strongly endorsed the role of Christian NGOs, and the role of spirituality in the development process. These are two of the 22 points contained in the final CIDA document, *Christian NGOs and CIDA: Guiding Principles, Understandings and Affirmations* (October 1995):

- 'CIDA recognises that faith-based organisations and institutions are an integral and legitimate part of a healthy and resilient civil society, and have an important role play in the development process.
- 'Christian NGOs believe that spirituality, belief systems, values and religion play an important role in the development process. CIDA also recognises that there is a spiritual dimension to the development process, and accepts that Christian NGOs and their southern partners often integrate this dimension into their relief and development programming' (CIDA 1995).

The 22 statements in the document address religion and development, evangelism and development, culturally sustainable development, partnership, women and visible minorities, and development education. While other governments, including the United Kingdom and Australia, followed this dialogue with interest, to my knowledge none has initiated a similar process.

Integrating gender issues into our work

The ways in which World Vision's Christian faith plays a part in the development process, and more specifically in gender and development, are as varied as our programmes. Most development practitioners would agree that a situation where culture or attitude denies basic human rights, or sustains misconceptions or ignorance, is not tolerable. At least half of those living in poverty are women and girls. Their poverty is perpetuated by the denial of access to resources and services, including education and health-care, and justified by culture and tradition. A concern for gender issues and women's poverty is therefore a concern about the roles and relationships which regulate women and men in their daily lives and about how these relationships support or subjugate, empower or deny the individual to engage fully in life – physically, socially, and spiritually.

In Tanzania during the early and mid-1990s, World Vision implemented a Child Survival Programme. During the final evaluation, carried out by Tanzanian staff, various members of the village were asked what impact the programme had on them. An old woman, gave a startling response. She said that as a result of the programme, old women were no longer being killed. In that region, when a child died, the parents paid a witch doctor for advice, who would blame the death on an old woman in the village, and state that unless she was killed other children in the family would be afflicted and die. Because the Child Survival Programme had greatly enhanced children's health and survival, very few old women were subsequently blamed and killed.

Staff in Tanzania felt they had to make a choice. Should they simply be thankful that the children were healthier, and that as a result, old women were no longer persecuted and killed? Or should they address a belief-system that killed innocent and vulnerable old women? They decided that the belief required a spiritual response. World Vision workers then began a dialogue with the leaders and people of that region, addressing the question of the value of a belief that required that old women be sacrificed to appease a spirit or break a curse. It is out of shared experiences and respect for one another that we can explore the root causes of many of the attitudes and traditions that keep women in a kind of bondage.

Integrating gender issues in World Vision and beyond

During the 1980s, many initiatives in all areas of World Vision's work aimed to address women's particular needs and issues, both at the programme level as well as within the organisation's structure. But it was not until 1989, thanks to the vision – and tenacity – of a few people, that gender issues became a priority for World Vision's Council and International Board. A Women's Commission was appointed. This was a body of ten staff, women and men drawn from field offices, senior management, and programme support. I had the privilege of being a member. Our mandate was threefold: first, to develop a policy that addressed the lack of women in leadership both in programming and organisational structure; second, to develop a strategy to implement the policy; and third, to write a theological reflection paper that would provide a biblical foundation for the policy. We wrote a devotional guide on women in the Bible for use in daily prayer groups, and produced a video and discussion guide that was sent to every office and Board with a draft policy for discussion. We invited feedback, and received volumes of responses. Clearly, we had touched a nerve.

Within two years, the Women's Commission had fulfilled its mandate. We developed a gender policy, and designed a strategy for implementation that acknowledged the diversity of cultural and legal systems within which World Vision offices operate. Our theological reflection paper was published as a study guide, *Women as Leaders*, based on the work of Katherine Haubert, a theological student at the time. Both the policy and the study guide were distributed throughout the World Vision Partnership.[4]

Implementation of our gender policy continues to be a slow process, involving awareness-building, attitudinal change, and resource-allocation, to ensure that the barriers and prejudices that prevent women from full participation are dismantled. The appointment last year of a Director of Gender and Development at the international level was an encouraging milestone: the incumbent is a woman, and she is from India. World Vision still has a long way to go in terms of creating a fully integrated organisation with respect to women in leadership and programmes. However, the policies are in place, and we are working on getting it right.

Using biblical evidence to promote gender equality

Going through the process of developing a policy on gender issues did not guarantee that this would be enacted across the organisation. Achieving an understanding of gender issues, and acting accordingly, is about more than legislating certain criteria or quotas. It is about a change in attitude. Given the diversity in cultures and Christian expression within the organisation, it would have been naïve to assume that everyone everywhere shared the same understanding. But given our common acceptance of Jesus' life and teachings as central to our organisational ethos, we could appeal to his treatment of and engagement with women as a basis for mutual discussion and learning.

Jesus is widely recognised, among Christians and others, as a wise and profound teacher. But he is rarely referred to as a feminist. However, he did repeatedly defy his own culture to support, heal, teach, and act as an advocate for women – often at his peril. He exposed the hypocrisy of those who would keep women subjugated, marginalised, and silent. His treatment of women challenged the status quo and put him at odds with Jewish traditions and laws.

Jesus challenging existing gender relations
In the Book of Mark, the Bible gives us an account of Jesus as a healer, curing a woman who had suffered from uncontrollable bleeding for 12 years (Mark 5, 25-34). It is likely that this woman lived in the shadows, bowed down, ashamed, avoiding the sneers of pity or disgust. It must have taken great courage for her to work her way through the

crowd, to touch the hem of Jesus' robe in the hope and faith that this action would heal her. This story demonstrates how Jesus defied Jewish laws on gender relations to meet a woman's needs – Jewish men were forbidden to speak with strange women in public, and any Jewish man touched by a woman who was menstruating was required to cleanse himself because women in this state were considered unclean.

In Mark's account, Jesus calls the woman to him, sensing that his robe had been touched. Frightened and trembling, she approaches. Falling before him, she admits it was she who touched him – but says that she has been healed. Jesus addresses her with tenderness, calling her his daughter, and tells her to 'go in peace, and be healed of your affliction'. Mark states that Jesus was on an important mission at the time of this encounter, going to the home of the ruler of the synagogue to heal his sick daughter. But he took the time to speak, to offer affirmation and encouragement to a woman who was without status or means. Culture and tradition do not take precedence in this story over giving a poor, outcast woman both the physical healing she needed, and the spiritual affirmation that her faith was important and that she should know peace in her life.

In line with this story, for over 25 years, World Vision has supported the Fistula Hospital in Addis Ababa, Ethiopia, where young women are healed of injuries and incontinence which are caused by protracted labour, and associated with early marriage and immature body development. The hospital is led by staff who believe that the surgery, as well as the emotional and mental support which they offer to fistula patients, is a practical act of love. They see themselves as being the hands and feet of Jesus, and doing what he would do.

Jesus promoting women's involvement in the 'public sphere'

An example of Jesus' attitudes to women's education, and their involvement in activities beyond the home, is given in the book of Luke (chapter 10, 38-42). In this account of Jesus as teacher, Mary and Martha are sisters who often opened their home to Jesus. Martha is anxious that Mary is spending time with Jesus, listening to his teaching, rather than helping her to prepare the meal. Jesus' response to her goes against the grain of gender norms in his society. Women were normally denied the lively debates that occupied men and religious leaders. In this story, Jesus says that what Mary has chosen to do, is not only necessary and positive, but that 'it will not be denied her'. In other words, she had a right to sit at the feet of the teacher. By declaring that Mary should be allowed to learn, to explore, and to expand her mind, Jesus was again setting a different course for women.

This account gives a powerful signal to Christians in modern society to promote education and participation in public life for women. The vast majority of children who are denied an education are girls, and the majority of illiterate adults are women (Leach 1998). Yet not only is education a human right of girls, it is a crucial means of breaking the poverty cycle. It has been stated many times that investing in girls' education is the most important investment the world can make. During 1998 World Vision had at least 75 projects in Africa, Asia, Latin America, the Middle East, and Eastern Europe which focused primarily on the girl child, or where the girl child was one specific programme component. These projects aim to enable thousands of girls to enrol and stay in school, avoiding early marriage and exploitative work, while developing skills that will allow them a greater degree of independence than their mothers.

Jesus addressing women's sexual exploitation

The Book of John (chapter 8, 2-11) offers an account of Jesus' advocacy on behalf of women involved in sexual activity which would normally be condemned by society. A woman caught in the act of adultery (sex outside marriage) is brought to Jesus; tradition dictates that she should be stoned to death. Jewish religious leaders wanted to use this occasion to trap Jesus into a direct challenge to this tradition. However, John tells us that Jesus turned the tables on the religious leaders. He refused to exonerate the woman, but at the same time demanded, 'he who is without sin should cast the first stone'. In doing so, he saved the woman's life. Then he went on to say that since the men no longer condemned her, shamed by the recognition of their own guilt, neither did Jesus. He ends the encounter by telling the woman to 'go and sin no more'.

When girls or women are forced into earning money by selling sexual services to survive, or are deceived and trafficked into such work, many lose their sense of dignity and self-worth. In working with street children and girls rescued from the sex trade, World Vision becomes their advocate against pimps and racketeers. Often, their emotional and psychological healing is enhanced by the knowledge of a loving and personal God. An example of this that will always stand out in my mind was an encounter I had with a woman from Labadi, a slum in Accra, Ghana, where World Vision funded a women's group to generate income through activities including baking bread, tie-dyeing textiles, and making charcoal. At one meeting I attended, this woman told her story:

'When Alice Yerenki came from World Vision offering to teach various skills that would allow us to abandon prostitution and earn money to feed and educate our children, I just laughed. This would be one more empty promise. All I had known was neglect, violence and abuse. Only my children kept me from suicide. Who would care for them? It took some time to convince me, but I finally decided to risk it, to believe that Alice really cared. It was like a small seed was planted inside, and I felt both hope and fear. But Alice kept her word. She taught me how to bake bread. Now I am earning money and I no longer prostitute myself to men who treat me like trash. My children are in school, and they are happy and healthy.' Then, as tears flowed down her scarred face, she said, 'But the most important thing Alice taught me is that God loves me. And now I know that when he looks at me he sees a beautiful flower.' This ability to overcome external obstacles and to discover one's inner strength, beauty, and dignity is what transformational development is all about.

Questioning misogyny justified by biblical evidence

One would be ill-advised to discuss the role of women in a Christian context and not mention the apostle Paul. Many of the arguments against women in leadership stem from particular interpretations of Paul's teaching. Much emphasis has been given in the past to Paul's statements about women submitting to husbands, keeping silent, and not teaching. However, for many women who are gifted and called to a ministry of teaching, preaching, and leadership, the growing body of literature interpreting Paul as a supporter of women is vindicating. Many scholars now argue that Paul acknowledged the role women played both in leadership and as friends and followers of Jesus, pointing to statements such as, 'there is no longer Jew nor Greek, slave nor free, male nor female – but we are all one in Christ' (Galatians 3, 26-29). The debate will continue in many fora – but in World Vision it is stated in key documents, including the Policy on Gender and Development, that we accept the giftedness of women equal to that of men and seek to benefit from all that women and men have to offer the work of bringing help and hope to suffering people.

Conclusions

Having gone through the process of developing our gender policy, I would offer two observations. From the outset, the governing bodies of the organisation agreed that the starting point for the policy was that God created women and men in his image – gifting both with skills to lead, teach, and preach. Having this fundamental position to work from spared the Women's Commission and the organisation long and painful debates about the role of women and their right to lead. We could get on with the task of actually developing policy and strategy.

The tension between policy and attitude is common to most efforts to achieve gender equality – Christian and non-Christian. But for management and staff working to promote gender issues within World Vision, being able to use Jesus' teaching and example has given credibility and strength to the organisation's commitment to gender equality. World Vision will continue to implement good development practices and gender-sensitive programmes. The combination of being Christian and struggling with the issue of gender equity allows World Vision to play a unique role in development, addressing the spiritual dimensions as well as the social and political. Christian beliefs are not a detriment to pursuing gender equity. In fact, they can be an asset.

Linda Tripp is Vice President of Advocacy and Government Relations at World Vision Canada. You can contact her at: World Vision Canada, 6630 Turner Valley Road, Mississauga, Ontario, Canada L5N 2S4. Phone: +1 (905) 821 3033 ext. 2713. Fax: +1 (905) 821 1825. E-mail: linda_tripp@worldvision.ca

References

Christian, J (1995) 'Rethinking a Christian response to the poor', paper written as part of a PhD thesis, Fuller Theological Seminary, California.

Leach, F (1998) 'Gender, education, and training: an international perspective' in *Gender and Development Vol. 6, No. 2, Education and Training,,* Oxfam GB: Oxford.

Notes

1 Here defined as development which addresses not just the physical circumstances of people's lives, but people's own perceptions of themselves, including of their value and worth as human beings. Development changes both external cicumstances and internal mind-sets, freeing people to realise their true potential.

2 Advocacy has become a significant focus of World Vision's work campaigning on issues such as the land mines, child sexual exploitation, the needs and rights of children of war, child soldiers, and girl children, and debt-forgiveness or debt-reduction of highly-indebted countries.

3 World Vision's total staff globally number just over 9000. Of these, only 402 are expatriates in their countries of work.

4 Copies are available from World Vision/MARC Publications, 800 West Chestnut Avenue, Monrovia, California 91016-3198. Phone: 626-301-7720; fax: 626-301-7786. Web site: http://www.marcpublications.com

Islam and development:

Opportunities and constraints for Somali women

Sadia Ahmed

Economic and social crisis can force communities to seek refuge in religious faith; in such situations, communities become more susceptible to the influence of groups which use religious beliefs as a means to gain power. Sadia Ahmed describes the effects on women's lives of the rise of Islamic extremism in Somalia since the early 1990s.

In 1991, after 21 years of Siyad Barre's dictatorial regime, social and political upheavals brought Somalia to its knees: civil strife shredded the country into factions and the government finally collapsed, with disastrous consequences (for an account of the conflict, see Bradbury 1994). The conflict had a profound effect on the lives of the Somali people by destroying traditional economic systems, thus challenging women and men to change their respective economic roles.

Over the past two decades, extreme Islamic movements have gained momentum in Somalia (as elsewhere). I will examine some of the consequences for women of the rise of such groups, based on research carried out in 1996 by a coalition of grassroots women's organisations in Somalia's capital, Mogadishu.

Challenges to gender relations

Somalia's economy is mainly dependent on pastoralism. In the rural areas, livestock trade continues to be the backbone of the economy. Before the war, women from pastoralist groups were not usually directly involved in market transactions, and women's role in the economy seemed less significant than was actually the case. However, when it became difficult for men to travel for fear of government troops, the task of marketing livestock and buying foodstuffs and other goods for the family was increasingly – and continues to be – left to women (Warsame 1998). In urban areas, too, women's role in the economy became more visible. Today, although their incomes are generally low and the majority of female entrepreneurs have little or no education, women are increasingly forced to become the main breadwinner. The collapse of government has led to widespread unemployment among civil servants, and has forced more women into the market-place, pressurised to meet their families' needs. The government was the main employer in Somalia; the voluntary and private sectors are relatively small.

The rise of religious extremism

The rise of religious extremist groups in Somalia began in the early 1970s, when the communist regime introduced the ideology of scientific socialism. A rebel movement promoting Islamic values arose; this was generally welcomed by people, who saw it as shoring up 'Somali' religious values and culture, and who felt a deep antipathy towards communism. Government crack-downs on this movement created further sympathy among the public, but over the years, support for Islamic groups has waned. Judging from my own conversations with Somalis, these groups are commonly perceived to be foreign-funded and programmed. People also think that their agendas are incompatible with the interests of the Somali state. Extremists' mistakes, such as openly showing disrespect towards well-respected religious institutions, have led to further disillusionment on the part of the public. It has not proved easy to impose an extremist agenda on people who have been practising Muslims for centuries.

However, extreme Islamists do retain much support among certain social groups. Over the past decade in particular, they have found a large number of young male and female supporters who have grown up with little experience of life beyond conflict, with high unemployment rates and a lack of alternatives due to the destruction of schools. It is a well-known fact among Somalis that some extremist religious groups create business and employment opportunities for loyal followers (personal communication, 1998).

The impact of Islamic extremism on Somali women

Hasan (1991) lists the central Islamic principles which have been compromised by extremist groups in their quest for popularity and power, and suggests that the issue of women's roles and women's rights is the only one on which such groups will not compromise: 'for them, women's liberation movements (or associations) are the central enemy, because the entire patriarchal society, whose existence fundamentalism has gone to the defence of, is built upon the oppression of women' (Hasan 1991, p35).

Throughout the conflict and afterwards, Somali women's organisations in different parts of the country have been active in both development work and advocacy for peace. Currently, women's groups are challenging both the government and NGOs to recognise and promote the role of women in society, and to resist threats to their rights. Challenges have been made by religious extremists to women's rights within marriage and the family, to their economic and political participation outside the home, and to their freedom of dress and behaviour.

In 1996, a coalition of women's grassroots organisations in Mogadishu conducted a study on Somali women's rights from the perspective of Islam. The study was motivated by a concern about the increasing number of fundamentalist movements mushrooming throughout the country, and the implications of this for women and development; about a perceived low awareness among Somali women on women's rights in Islam; and about the tendency of groups of educated men to retain information or blatantly mislead women about their rights and duties.

The study was conducted using questionnaires of mainly closed-ended questions, designed to explore the level of respondents' awareness regarding women's rights. 120 people (80 women and 40 men from local communities) were interviewed. The findings confirmed that many women are confused about their rights, obligations, and duties as articulated in Islam. It also highlighted the fact that wholesome and unwholesome traditional practices tend to be associated with Islam, and with women's rights as defined in Islam. It reconfirmed that violations against Somali women's rights are culturally rooted, and that such practices continue unchecked (Sheck et. al. 1996).

Marriage and the family

The widespread practice of relatively late marriage in Somalia is under threat. The national planning statistics of 1988 recorded the average age of marriage as 21 for girls, and 25 for boys; as more young people sought university education, the age of marriage was further postponed. However, this trend has been reversed by the collapse of the educational system. As fundamentalism strengthens its hold on the community, boys and girls are encouraged to marry ever earlier.

The Islamic principle of male responsibility for the family's maintenance, as outlined in the Q'uran (Afshar 1998), is being seriously undermined by young men being encouraged to marry one or more wives without economic means. The research confirmed that many young girls are ultimately either deserted or divorced. Since young couples sometimes marry without the parents' consent, deserted or divorced wives cannot always count on the support they could have otherwise relied on within the extended family system.

The research also suggests that ignorance of what the Q'uran says regarding polygamy is creating a problem for women. In 1998, I personally heard of a young girl under 20 with three children and little means, who was informed that her husband had married another woman; she calmly listened and defended him, saying 'it is his right' (personal communication, Sept 1998). In fact, the Q'uran sets out men's responsibility in single or polygamous marriages: polygamy is only permissible under strict social circumstances; it is therefore a conditional permission and not an article of faith or mortal necessity (Sheck et. al. 1996).

Another development issue affecting women in their role within the family is fertility and family-planning. Spacing children is not a subject entertained by fundamentalists, despite the fact that the Q'uran encourages it; Islam gives women a wide range of rights, and does not oppose family-planning, especially when women's health is at stake. Early and frequent child-bearing increases young women's health risks.

Political and economic participation
Since the end of the war, Somalia has seen a decline of women's power in formal politics. The new political structures are principally based on clan relationships; it is becoming increasingly evident that unless parties free from clan politics are established, and the present strategy of fostering clan representation, common all over Somalia, is revisited, women's participation in politics will continue to be severely hampered. In Somaliland, as in Somalia, groups in power are using religion as the basis for excluding women from politics. A colleague who chairs the Umbrella Women's Organisation in Hargeisa, Somaliland, recounted to me that every time they organised a workshop, the Minister of Justice and Religious Affairs came to interrogate participants about their activities, until he was officially asked by Parliament to stop this. He stated that his actions were based on his belief that women can be easily influenced by foreigners, and hence felt they needed protection (personal communication, 1998).

Veiling and control of behaviour
In Somalia, a society at war with itself, and where sexual violation has also become a tool of war, the tendency towards more extreme religious practice has been reinforced by the perceived need for protection and protective clothing. The number of veiled women in Somalia has visibly increased since 1991. Somali women's traditional dress is modest, but allows them freedom of movement and is thus more practical than the veil. As a Somali woman, I have seen that the recent increase in veiling has been accompanied, for the first time in Somali history, with extreme forms of censorship of women's behaviour, as extreme versions of Islamic interpretation have found fertile ground. Women who refuse to conform are harassed by both sexes, and peer pressure is exerted on them to veil.

Religious education and women's rights

Lack of religious education among the public allows extremists to use Islamic texts against women. Hadiths[1] are among the strongest weapons used to justify the marginalisation of Muslim women from religious and social power. Although a significant portion of the accounts of the Prophet's comments and deeds was recounted on the authority of women, (Ahmed 1990), the Hadiths were written by men. Many Hadiths that undermine women's freedom actually contradict the actions and philosophy of the Prophet Mohammed; the misogyny employed in the collection of such Hadiths has been discussed elsewhere (Mernissi 1991, Ahmed 1990). In addition, the fact that Arabic is not widely spoken in Somalia helps religious extremists to maintain their hold over communities: for example, they justify ideas about the weakness of women by arguing that the Arabic word *al nisaa* (the female) is synonymous with the Arabic word *nisf* (half). Through such arguments, women and men are made to believe that women are less intelligent in the eyes of Allah, and that the limitation of their rights is therefore justified. Until Somali women receive a better education, and better religious education in particular, this situation looks set to continue. Women's organisations are the only part of civil society to attempt seriously to redress the extremists' strategy of marginalising women on the grounds of religious 'evidence'.

While the challenge of research and work by women's organisations is significant enough to cause concern to religious extremists and their supporters, their work is hindered by the lack of a coherent shared policy, and lack of access to the growing literature by Islamic scholars of both sexes, which challenges the denial of women's rights using religious texts. Women's organisations must bring about coherence in policy and achieve improved cooperation in designing and implementing strategies to challenge the erosion of women's rights.

Formerly the Director of the Women's Research Unit at the Somali Academy of Sciences and Arts, Somalia, Sadia Ahmed now works as gender co-ordinator for the Pastoral and Environmental Network in the Horn of Africa (PENHA). Contact her at PENHA, PO Box 494, 1 Laney House, Portpool Lane, London EC1N 7FP. E-mail: p.PENHA@ukonline.co.uk.

References

Ahmed L, 'Women and the Advent of Islam' in *Women under Muslim Law*, Dossier 7/8, France, 1991.

Al Bushra, J and Piza-Lopez, E (1994) 'Gender, War and Food' in *War and Hunger: Rethinking International Responses to Complex Emergencies*, SCF and Zed Books: London.

Baden S (1992) The Position of Women in Islam Countries: Possibilities, Constraints and Strategies for Change, report prepared for special programme, WID, Netherlands Ministry of Foreign Affairs (DGIS), Bridge.

Bradbury, M (1994) *The Somali Conflict: prospects for peace*, Oxfam GB: Oxford.

Hasan, M (1991) 'On fundamentalism on our Land' in *Women living under Muslim Law*, Dossier 11/12/13.

http://www.submission.org/hom.htm# WOM, Musjid Tuscon, USA, 1998.

Mernissi, F (1991) *The Veil and the Male Elite: A Feminist Interpretation of Women's rights in Islam*, Addison-Wesley: UK.

Ragab N (1997) The Record Set Straight: Women in Islam Have Rights, an internet report, Islam (Submission to God) Web page, Musjid Tuscon, United Submitters International, USA.

Sheck, M, Ibrahim, H, Abdi A, Mohamed, F (1996) Report on Somali Women's Rights from the Perspective of Islam, NOVIB report, Mogadishu.

Warsame A (1998) The Civil War in Somalia: Differential Impact on Women and Men, paper presented at a workshop on Resource Competition in Eastern Africa organised by the Institute of Social Studies (ISS) and OSSREA, 12-13 August 1998.

Notes

1 Reported accounts of the life of the Prophet Mohammed.

'The way to do is to be':

Exploring the interface between values and research

Sharon Harper and Kathleen Clancy

A project run by the Canadian International Development Research Centre brought together a wide variety of specialists in order to explore the links between gender, science, and development, and to shape holistic, 'being-oriented' approaches, where values based in religion and spirituality inform the perspective and choices of methods of development researchers and practitioners.

'People have to see with new eyes, and understand with new minds, before they can truly turn to new ways of living. The most important change that people can make is to change their way of looking at the world. We can change studies, jobs, neighbourhoods, even countries and continents, and still remain much as we always were. But change our fundamental angle of vision, and everything changes – our priorities, our values, our judgments, our pursuits. Again and again, in the history of religion, this total upheaval in the imagination has marked the beginning of a new life ... a turning of the heart, a "metanoia," by which men [sic] see with new eyes and understand with new minds, and turn their energies to new ways of living.' (Barbara Ward, as quoted in Commission on Global Governance, 1995)

Barbara Ward's insight, like the title of this article, 'the way to do is to be,' (attributed to the ancient Taoist master Lao Tse), offers an intriguing challenge to traditional development methodologies. This article describes the Science, Religion, and Development (SRD) project of the International Development Research Centre (IDRC),

a Canadian federally-funded research for development organisation. The SRD project aims to illuminate other realms of knowledge which we believe to be complementary to gender, science, and development perspectives, and to show the links between these perspectives. The SRD project might also be considered a step in the evolution of emerging approaches on development and research, which we call 'being-oriented'[1], and which are characterised by their reference to religion and spirituality.

In this article, we attempt to show how many of the values that underlie the use of gender analysis as a tool in research for development are similar to values behind these 'being-oriented approaches.' It is well-known that new ways of understanding the social construction of people's roles, experiences, and relationships can lead to new ways of doing research (Kirby 1989). For example, by emphasising the importance of the socially-constructed relations between men and women, gender-sensitive approaches have enabled researchers to consider different realms of experience, and this has opened up new possibilities for study (see F

Steady 'The Inadequacy of the Dominant Research Methodology,' as quoted in Connelly et al. 1996). We suggest here that 'being-oriented approaches' offer similar new possibilities for researchers. As we discuss, however, there are also some essential differences between gender-sensitive approaches to research and being-oriented approaches; we attempt here to show how the broader context and the additional values offered by 'being-oriented approaches' have the potential to transform research for development.

Our background

We are, respectively, the project and programme officers of the SRD project, but the opinions and observations expressed here are our own. While we personally both recognise a spiritual dimension to living, and carry this into our work in the SRD project, we also recognise that religion can be associated with some of the worst abuses in human history, and a number of current situations of war and civil strife. Religions can reinforce fatalism, encourage division (some religious groups use development work as a weapon in the competition for adherents), and impose rigid dogmas on attempts at change (Lean 1995). Religions have not necessarily been the mouthpiece or friend of marginalised groups, including women, and have on occasion been instrumental in suppressing those voices and in paving the way for oppressive regimes.

Nor, in considering the issue of religion in relation to science and development, do we give up the 'mantle of reason' regarding our commitment to methods of experimentation and observation. Rather, we are questioning whether an important perspective has been left out of the debates on, and methodologies for, research for development; and we question what consequences this may have had for the quality of interventions made in the name of development and/ or in the advancement of science. Like gender studies, science, religion, and development studies are all informed by value-systems which serve particular social, political, and economic interests, and any value system in research for development[2] can be applied judicious or injudiciously. We believe that the values behind the 'being-oriented approaches' we explore here could enhance the quality of development research and practice, by offering access to expanded sets of values and points of view.

The SRD project

The Science, Religion, and Development (SRD) project stems from preliminary research carried out by William F Ryan, an economist and a Jesuit priest (Ryan 1995). In an attempt to move beyond economistic understandings of development, and to identify the conceptual and practical linkages between science, religion, and development, Ryan travelled to developing countries and interviewed more than 180 informants, who combined one or more of the roles of scientists, development workers, and people of faith. Based on this initial research, an international workshop was held in August 1995 in Val Morin, Quebec. Participants agreed that the issues uncovered were significant factors in the effectiveness of future development interventions in their countries, and they urged IDRC to continue the research[3]. The SRD project has three phases.

In the first phase, IDRC brought together a core group of four individuals: experts in science, international development, or theology, each from a different cultural and religious background. Together and separately, this core group has worked to reflect, from their different cultural, religious, and professional positions, on the relationship between the moral/ spiritual realms of life and the technological/scientific models of development. Consider this interaction, they have attempted to identify the effect that this interaction has had for development discourse and practice. Questions of how development can be environmentally sustainable, and achieve equality between women and men, are central to these discussions.

The core group found that their initial reflections had led to a focus on different aspects of development; however, each group member had amalgamated the personal and the professional, using their individual faiths to question and illuminate their separate areas of scientific enquiry. The core group saw their research papers as experimental steps towards a new type of integrated and engaged scholarship, and towards the introduction of a new perspective in broader debates on international development. These reflections included considerations such as the ambiguity of religion[4] and the role of religion in promoting humility and self-limitation on the part of researchers and workers within science and development.

The second and third phases will include the publication of these reflections in book form. In addition, in conjunction with the core group, IDRC plans to widen the circle involved in the project to an extended network of researchers who write and practice in relevant areas of development. The aim will be to stimulate further debate about the questions addressed in Phase 1, and to elicit further reflections from the points of view of other faiths and scientific backgrounds. The extended network will add legitimacy to the work and provide access for its concepts into other areas of development.

Religion, institutions, and belief systems

In the SRD project, we aim to deal with religious content, not religious institutions. Religion as content 'has to do with the idea of the supreme, the supernatural which organises the world and connects people through language and practice to what is considered the inviolable, the sacrosanct' (Haynes 1996). As a result of the legitimisation of unequal power structures often associated with religion, however, a number of people who encounter the SRD project reject its premise outright, or prefer to use terms such as 'spirituality' or 'human values', to dissociate the project from these injustices.

Remnants of our own struggle with the terms and concepts of religion and spirituality have remained throughout the project, and provide an example of its evolutionary and participatory process. For example, at its inception, the project was called 'Human Values and Belief Systems'; Ryan's book explicitly uses the term 'spirituality' in the title. The value of 'spirituality' is that it allows for the consideration of belief systems, such as the animistic beliefs prevalent in many countries, which do not fit within the category of organised religion. However, focusing on organised religion allows us to consider thought-structures and approaches which can be compared with scientific methods, and we can distinguish at a basic level between personal interpretation, historical ethos, social organisation, and religious tenets. However, the project's emphasis on the participants' reflections and their internal synthesis of science, religion, and development ensures that spirituality is not excluded or over-whelmed by the formality of religion.

'Being-oriented' approaches: a comparison with other methodologies

Many of the underlying values in approaches based on ethics, social justice, and gender-awareness are shared by 'being-oriented' approaches. In this section, we use the case of the SRD project to illustrate a few points of similarity, and highlight some differences.

By presenting evidence which supports the aim of transforming inequitable relations between women and men, gender-sensitive research is designed to feed into an agenda for change (Kabeer 1996). This research agenda displays a strong concern for the values and principles articulated in the Universal Declaration of Human Rights, including equality, justice, solidarity, inclusion, diversity, inter-connectedness, social awareness, personal integrity, and the dignity and worth of every person regardless of his or her differences. These values inform gender-aware researchers' choice of areas of study and methods.

In examining social roles and relationships of women and men, most gender-sensitive research considers other criteria such as race, class, religion, caste, age, physical/ mental abilities, marital status, sexual orientation and attributes which describe, to the fullest extent possible, the vast diversity of the human condition. Inclusion of different perspectives in the research process is an overt value, as well as a goal in itself, of gendered research. Participatory methods also espouse the values of inclusion and the dignity and worth of every person, and aim to ensure that typically marginalised perspectives are included in the research process (Holland 1995; Kirby 1989)[5]

Similarly, the values and methodology of the SRD project display a concern for inclusion and authentic dialogue (although this commitment is far from perfectly enacted). The SRD research agenda was collaboratively set, through open-ended enquiry with participants. IDRC consciously tried to decrease the power differential that usually exists between donors and researchers; the core group of researchers, to a large extent, determined the process and decided to use non-conventional research techniques. Particular attention was given to the importance of women's voices, voices from the South, and representation from a variety of religions in convening the core group for Phase 1; as the project progresses, these concerns for inclusion and participation will continue as new participants are invited to join. Participants in the SRD project also bring these concerns for inclusion and solidarity with them, from participating in social justice causes, and working with groups which address the needs of the marginalised.[6]

The SRD project also shares with gender-sensitive research a commitment to transparency about the assumptions and biases that are present in all research. Transparency by the researcher contributes to clarity about the research questions, goals, and methods, and can be instrumental in avoiding the perpetuation of inequalities. One controversial research method which embraces this value is 'reflexivity', in which researchers collect field notes which monitor their own reactions to the research process. (Kirby 1989; Holland 1995; Bell 1993). Here, all assumptions and beliefs regarding the research throughout the research cycle are recorded and contemplated. Where relevant, these notes can be included at the recording stage of the research. Through this process, researchers are required to question and articulate clearly their own standpoints and assumptions; this also allows them to be challenged, by the researchers themselves and, ultimately, by others. Reflexivity can help the researcher engage more fully with the people with whom they work, going beyond the interaction characteristic of traditional academic research. (Yano 1997)

A reflexive approach emerged for the SRD project, because questions of faith usually operate at a personal level. The project required a methodology that would allow participants to put personal beliefs into words, and make this explicit for other researchers. Participants encouraged each other to reflect upon, and write, accounts of how their faith operated in their own professional lives, and thus in the mechanisms of their development work. Their personal and subjective experiences vis-à-vis the project's research questions were explicitly valued and sought out during the process. We from IDRC became conscious, during this process, of our situation within the group's dynamics, and tried not to impose our own ideas and concerns about how the research should proceed. In this way, IDRC tried to be open when the researchers questioned cherished assumptions, values, and approaches of the research for development community.

Values specific to 'being-oriented' approaches

In the process of preparing for this article, we also tried to identify some assumptions and values that could be said to be specific to 'being-oriented' approaches (of which the SRD is an early example). We were looking for values that could be specifically attributed to the researcher's experience of faith (whether through organised religion, or personal spirituality). We wanted to see how these might be manifested in the professional lives of the SRD participants, and how they might have informed the project itself. This was not an easy task because, in almost every case, one of us would mention a value that seemed implicit in a 'being-oriented' approach, only to find that it had reflections and refractions in gender-aware and/or participatory research principles and techniques.

We did identify one significant difference with a number of implications, although for some it may seem a difference of degree rather than of kind. People of religious faith or spirituality have a relationship with a transcendental reality – a perception of guiding principles that underlie 'reality' – which offers a broad context for understanding human actions. In contrast, approaches within development may advocate values such as justice, dignity, fairness, and equality, but these tend to be understood as operating only with reference to the world's political, economic, and social systems – the 'here and now' – and on a relatively traditional understanding of the principles of human interaction. Approaches drawing from religion and spirituality might ask where one can find an ultimate reference point, or deeper principles, in which to base these values, and through which these principles of interaction can be revisualised.[7]

The concept of human well-being that is a fundamental goal of development can, and must, include intangible concepts such as creating, connection, belonging, love, and hope, which are rooted in a relationship or perception of reality that goes beyond the here-and-now. 'Being-oriented' approaches take into account that people can act for change from a desire to attain meaning and fulfilment, as well as from an understandable desire for change in their material circumstances. As Mary Lean wrote in her book on spiritually oriented development approaches: '[D]evelopment that is grounded

in faith has two outstanding advantages. It builds on a community's deepest sense of identity and belonging, and it carries within it the seeds of individual empowerment.' (Lean 1995, 10).

'Being-oriented' approaches to human development could therefore subtly expand a number of the values we have identified as underlying gendered approaches. One may, for example, research the causes of and solutions to gender-based violence in a war-torn country, based on a desire to alleviate injustices, inequalities, poverty, and suffering, without recourse to any of these 'transcendental' principles of reality. But, in their absence, how do development researchers and workers understand the need for mental and spiritual healing through reconciliation? Without some understanding of a larger purpose or context for their lives and actions, how can people risk the forgiveness and reconciliation necessary to rebuild a community out of chaos? How do researchers and development workers find the strength not to retreat from the realities of the people with whom they are working? And how can they articulate these needs or integrate these understandings into a list of solutions without understanding or using this language and these concepts?

Alternative approaches to research and development based in religion or spirituality would enable us to value and work with concepts that are rarely expressed in gender-sensitive research, such as forgiveness and reconciliation, compassion, empathy, wisdom (as complementary to knowledge), non-violence, sacrifice,[8] self-limitation, simplicity, kindness, and connection. Consideration for these concepts carries practical consequences for researchers and workers in development. For example, one SRD participant pointed out that there is a difference between the 'preferential option for the poor' originating in Latin American Catholicism and the Marxism with which it has been associated: Marxism, he argued, outlines a preferential option for the proletariat. The difference between the orientations may appear slight, but could be seen in practice after the Nicaraguan revolution, when Christian-based communities did not favour punishment of Somoza's soldiers, wanting them to be forgiven and integrated into the community (personal communication, 1999)[9]

Of course, there are infinite variations on these themes. Differences of approach and ethos among and within religions challenge 'being-oriented' approaches to be open to values from every tradition. For example, in certain traditions, such as Buddhism, the concept of interconnectedness[10] is articulated as a 'principle of non-duality': all beings, and the environment in which they live, are fundamentally interrelated and inter-dependent. Interconnectedness is both a value and a basic organising principle of reality. Researchers and development workers could draw on this concept to recognise the networks of relationships they find in communities and to value these connections. They might use this principle to evaluate their methods, asking themselves whether a given approach will build and balance existing relationships or increase conflict and create new, if different, hierarchies (Yano 1997, 94-97).

Choosing a 'being-oriented' approach does not guarantee a certain way of thinking and acting, any more than sensitivity to gender issues predicts a particular approach. The point is that religiously or spiritually based approaches can provide an awareness of a frame of reference larger or deeper than the visible, material world, and thereby offer new possibilities for response, transforming the researchers themselves, and their understanding of and behaviour toward the communities with whom they work.

Conclusion: SRD, values, and methodology

We have discussed how values based in religion and spirituality can inform the perspective and choices of methods of development researchers and practitioners. But what new tools can 'being-oriented'

approaches show to be useful in the gathering of data and its analysis?

A number of traditions postulate that the only way to effect appropriate outward, social transformation (or development) is through personal self-transformation. Researchers and workers with a 'being-oriented' approach might engage in forms of contemplation, meditation, or prayer. The goals of these activities could include inspiration, self-knowledge, and self-acceptance (leading to compassion for others) as necessary corollaries to attempts to effect change in others. In addition, when researchers have access to relevant religious and inspirational texts and stories, they could include enquiries about rituals, myths, and parables in their work, not from the point of view of anthropologists analysing cultural manifestations, but as an attempt to challenge their own predetermined conceptions of the research process.

How does the convergence of the 'being-oriented' values and methods manifest itself in the SRD project? It is a research project based on what we know and how we do things now. On the face of it, holding conferences, maintaining a dialogue, and writing papers are not unusual, but our project is extraordinary in its recognition that something intangible, but important, is being left out of the development equation, and in its openness to different processes in investigating that missing element. If the experiment of the SRD project has lessons to offer, much of the credit must go to the two men and two women who make up the core group; they have applied the rich resources of their professional skills, their personal faiths, and their sceptical minds to this project. Primarily, each has worked out of love for the ideas of the project, and out of a belief that the project could provide valuable insights into the achievement of a deeper and wiser standard for human well-being[11]. There were moments of serendipity when the dialogue became too abstract, which IDRC could never have anticipated or scheduled, but which illustrate the potential for linking values with research methodology; at these times, the participants kept the process honest, grounded, and focussed on the realities of people living in extreme poverty. Another lesson from SRD includes the consideration and kindness which the participants showed each other, both within and outside of the meetings; the respect they show for their different traditions even during the most intense dialogue; their alternative but grounded perspectives which helped question the basic assumptions of traditional development models; and the trust, vulnerability, and courage they displayed in agreeing to speak and write personally about their beliefs, in the face of an academic establishment that is not accustomed to discussing personal, much less religious, orientations. The project has demonstrated to us that a wide range of opinions, views, and strongly held beliefs does not mean the end of community: in fact, acknowledging and respecting diverse views challenges our commitment to unity in diversity and can provide us with a multiplicity of resources.

Sharon Harper and Kathleen Clancy can be contacted via The Editor, Gender and Development or by e-mailing: SHarper@idrc.ca

References

Bell, D, Caplan, P, Karim, W (eds.) (1993) *Gendered Fields: Women, Men and Ethnography*, Routledge: New York.

Commission on Global Governance (1995) *Our Global Neighbourhood*, Oxford University Press: New York.

Connelly, MP, MacDonald, M, Murray Li, T, Parpart, J (1996) 'Theoretical Perspectives on Feminism and Development,' in *Theoretical Perspectives on Gender and Development*, The Commonwealth of Learning: Vancouver.

Haynes, J (1996) *Religion and Politics in Africa*, Zed: London.

Holland, J, Blair, M, Sheldon, S (eds.) (1995) *Debates and Issues in Feminist Research and Pedagogy*, The Open University: Bristol.

Kabeer, N, Ramya, S (1996) *Institutions, Relations and Outcomes: Framework and Tools for Gender-Aware Planning*, International Development Studies: UK.

Kirby, S, McKenna, K (1989) *Experience, Research, Social Change: Methods from the Margins*, Garamond Press: Toronto.

Lean, M (1995) *Bread, Bricks, and Belief: Communities in Charge of Their Future*, Kumarian: West Hartford.

Mayoux, L (1995) 'Beyond Naivety: Women, Gender Inequality and Participatory Development' in *Development and Change*, Vol. 26, pp. 235-258.

Ryan, WF (1995) *Culture, Spirituality, and Economic Development: Opening a Dialogue*, IDRC Books: Ottawa.

Steady, F (1983) 'Research Methodology and Investigative Framework for Social Change: The Case for African Women', seminar, Association of African Women for Research on Development, Dakar, 1983.

White, SC (1996) 'Depoliticising development: the uses and abuses of participation,' in *Development in Practice*, Vol. 6, pp. 6-15, Carfax: Abingdon.

Yano, S (1997) 'Alternative Visions of Development in Rural Thailand', unpublished paper submitted for a Master of Science to the University School for Rural Planning and Development, University of Guelph, Ontario, Canada.

Notes

1 We use this term cautiously and experimentally; perhaps there should not be one term that encompasses all these investigations into the meaning of existence, but simplicity of expression compelled us to try to find some term. We tested many possibilities. However, we liked 'being-oriented approaches' because, while it concentrates the attention on ultimate questions surrounding existence, it also seems to encompass naturalistic and supernaturalistic views of the universe; the environment and animals, as well as humans; and the fundamental juxta-

position between an existence based on having and acquiring and an existence in which the imperative is to be and to become according to one's fullest potential. We welcome suggestions for a better term.

2 See note 9.

3 The SRD project mirrors IDRC's own way of working: within the organisation's programmes, researchers from many disciplines are invited to bring their particular science and experience to bear on managing research for development. However, the SRD project differs from this internal IDRC experiment in one important way: it is constructed to accommodate and benefit from a range of scientific disciplines, but it also extends beyond the scientific mainstream to welcome perspectives based on particular expressions of faith.

4 See note 9.

5 Although done poorly, participatory research methods can further exacerbate the situation of women and other marginalised groups (White 1996, Mayoux 1995).

6 It is acknowledged that the SRD project is not working directly with grassroots groups but with individuals active within these groups.

7 Moving away from conflictual or competitive models of interaction towards those which encourage community and peacebuilding.

8 The concept of 'sacrifice' excited much debate among SRD participants, which points to the inherent ambiguity surrounding some of these concepts and values. Some participants felt that a rationale of 'sacrifice' is too often used to justify sacrifices on the part of the world's poorest and most marginalised people. Others felt that 'sacrifice' in the sense of 'self-limitation' or 'self-restraint' was a necessary concept for the North to understand, given the excesses of Northern lifestyles which are linked both to ecological degradation and poverty in the South.

9 For well-known examples of human-development initiatives that find inspiration in religion and/or spirituality, see the Alternatives to Consumerism Network (Thailand), the Sarvodaya Shramadana Movement (Sri Lanka) and the Swadhyaya Movement (India). Other examples are described in Lean 1995.

10 The concept of interconnectedness is not unknown in gender and development research and work, but it tends to focus on the connections between material resources and deprivation in networks of relationships such as communities and families.

11 The religious expression 'calling' was applied by a few to describe how they were drawn to participate in the project.

Resources

Compiled by Sophie Dodgeon

Books

Through the Devil's Gateway: Women, Religion and Taboo, Alison Joseph, Society for Promoting Christian Knowledge, in association with Channel Four Books, 1990.
A fascinating and wide-ranging selection of writings based on the 1990 television series of the same name. Among other topics, writers consider how women have been labelled 'impure', and look at Goddess-worship in India, and nineteenth-century medicine in relation to European women. They argue that religious traditions are at least able to admit the power of women's cycles of fertility, while secular society maintains an embarrassed silence about them.

Fundamentalism and Gender, John Stratton Hawley (ed.), 1994, Oxford University Press, Oxford and New York. 20 Madison Avenue, New York, 10016, USA.
The book's central theme is that religious fundamentalism is concerned with social structures, not with religious texts. These fascinating articles focus on Islam, Hinduism, the New Religions of Japan, and American Christianity, revealing that control over women is central to the funda-mentalist agenda in each of these religions.

Identity Politics and Women: cultural reassertions and feminisms in perspective, Valentine Mohgadam (ed.), 1994. Westview Press, 5500 Central Avenue, Boulder, Colorado 80301-2877, USA.
Fax +1 (303) 449 3356
Considers the rise of political and cultural movements which are bidding for political power, legal changes, or cultural supremacy, basing their claims on notions of religious, ethnic, and national identity. From examining such movements' attitudes to women, and attempts to control female freedom and sexuality through invoking Woman as a cultural symbol, the book moves to assess women's responses. Uses 13 case studies from Muslim, Christian, Jewish, and Hindu societies.

Reproductive Health Matters, Number 8: Fundamentalism, Women's Empowerment and Reproductive Rights, 1996.
29-35 Farringdon Road, London EC1 3JB.
This is a themed issue of the twice-yearly journal which concentrates on identifying and understanding women's reproductive health needs. Among the contributions are an examination of how women's reproductive rights are affected by Hindu nationalism, by charismatic and Pentecostal Christian move-ments in Brazil, by Roman Catholicism in Poland, and by Islam in Iran and Indonesia.

Women, Religion and Development in the Third World, Theodora Foster Carroll, 1983, Praeger Publishers. 88 Post Road, Westport, CT 06881, USA.

A comprehensive study of the position of women in Christianity, Islam, Hinduism, and Buddhism, giving an overview of each religion's key tenets, as well as accounts of policies on women's education and 'population' (sexuality and reproductive rights). The book places each religious tradition in its historical and social context, and suggests that religions could function as agents for change, rather than forces for regression. Written 15 years ago, this book, while containing thoroughly researched and very useful information, frequently resorts to judgemental language which may alienate some readers.

Women, Religion and Sexuality: Studies on the Impact of Religious Teachings on Women, Jeanne Becher (ed.), 1990, World Council of Churches Publications. PO Box 2100, 150 Rue de Ferney, 1211 Geneva 2, Switzerland.

A collection of 12 papers which were the outcome of a study of the main world religions and their attitudes to female sexuality. Most papers are followed by a short response from the same faith tradition which aims to increase dialogue within this tradition. Indigenous beliefs are also touched upon. A clear and accessible book which offers much to debate.

Speaking of Faith: Cross-Cultural Perspectives on Women, Religion and Social Change, Diana L Eck and Devaki Jain, 1986, The Women's Press, London.

Also available from Kali for Women, B1/8 Hauz Khas, New Delhi, 110 016, India.

Originally presented to a conference on the same theme, these papers consider how religion influences the kinds of social change which women are engaged in. They cover a wide range of traditions and countries, including papers on Ghandian ethics, Japanese traditions, and witches in Ghana. It suggests that both 'women' and 'religion' are the missing factors in development.

Women as Teachers and Disciples in Traditional and New Religions, Elizabeth Puttick and Peter B Clarke (eds.), 1993, Edwin Mellen Press, UK, Canada, USA.

Ten essays discussing how spiritual discipleship affects women. The essays ask whether discipleship implies a model of female submission, or whether it can in fact be empowering. Covers diverse traditions, such as Zen Buddhism, Afro-Brazilian religion, and modern paganism.

Islam and Feminisms: An Iranian Case-study, Haleh Afshar, 1998, Macmillan, Houndmills, Basingstoke, Hants RG21 6XS, UK.

Haleh Afshar gives a detailed and scholarly account of the strategies employed by Iranian women to maintain, and regain, their rights in present-day Iran. Afshar argues that it is no longer possible to disregard these strategies and denigrate Iranian women as powerless in the face of 'fundamentalism'. Feminism must learn to accommodate not only differences in opinion, but differences in strategy according to women's specific geographical and historical context.

Women and Gender in Islam: Historical roots of a modern debate, Leila Ahmed, 1992, Yale University Press, New Haven and London.

Explores the historical roots of the current debates on women and Islam by tracing the developments in Islamic discourses on women and gender from the ancient world to the present.

Muslim Women and the Politics of Participation: Implementing the Beijing Platform, Mahnaz Afkhami and Erika Friedl (eds.), 1997, Syracuse University Press, USA.

This collection of essays looks at ways of implementing the recommendations of the UN Fourth World Conference on Women in Muslim societies. The book is in three parts, examining theoretical views of women's rights within Muslim societies, practical ways to help women exercise their rights, and the role of international organisations in helping women.

Women and Islam in Muslim Societies, Hans Thijssen (ed.), Poverty and Development: Analysis and Policy series No. 7, Development Cooperation Information Department, 1994.
Ministry of Foreign Affairs, PO Box 20061, 2500 EB, The Hague, The Netherlands.
Part of a series examining poverty as a global phenomenon, published by the Development Cooperation Information Department in the Netherlands. With sections on women in Islamic jurisprudence, diversity in practice in different countries, case studies of six countries, a study of Muslim immigrant women in the Netherlands, and the transcript of a seminar on 'Women, Islam and Development', held in 1993.

Religion, Dress and the Body, Linda Boynton Arthur (ed.), 1999, Berg Publishers, 150 Cowley Road, Oxford, OX4 1JJ, UK
Explores how people express themselves through dress, despite religious constraints.

Servants of the Buddha: Winter in a Himalayan Convent, Anna Grimshaw, 1992, Open Letters. 147 Northchurch Road, London N1 3NT, UK.
A personal account of an extraordinary winter spent in a convent in Ladakh. It looks at the ambiguous position of women in a Buddhist society from a European perspective, and gives a detailed description of their lives and practices.

Standing Again at Sinai: Judaism from a Feminist Perspective, Judith Plaskow, 1991, Harper: SanFrancisco.
Refusing to believe that her Jewish and feminist selves cannot be reconciled, Judith Plaskow sets out her ideas for transforming Judaism through a feminist vision. With sections on the Torah, the idea of Israel, images and language associated with God, and a theology of sexuality.

Living Letters: a report of visits to the churches during the Ecumenical Decade – Churches in Solidarity with Women, World Council of Churches (WCC) Publications, 1997.
PO Box 2100, 1211 Geneva 2, Switzerland.

A multi-authored report of the process described in Bridget Walker's article in this issue of *Gender and Development*.

No Longer a Secret: the church and violence against women, Aruna Gnanadason,1996, WCC Publications.
'An unforgiving confrontation of the church's silence about violence against women, and a useful survey of the social and theological issues' (Crosslight). This book points to signs of hope as women and men in the church and elsewhere are beginning to struggle against all forms of violence against women.

Women, violence and non-violent change, Aruna Gnanadason, Musimbi Kanyoro and Lucia Ann McSpadden (eds.), 1995, WCC Publications.
This collection of analytical essays and case studies shows what contribution women are making towards conflict resolution in many different contexts. Authors come from across the world.

The power we celebrate: women's stories of faith and power, Musimbi Kanyoro and Wendy S Robbins (eds.), 1992, WCC Publications.
This book offers suggestions for empowering women to 'challenge oppressive structures in the global community, their country and their church'.

Women Healing Earth, Rosemary Radford Ruether (ed.), 1996, SCM Press, by arrangement with Orbis books. Orbis Books, Box 302, New York, 10545-0302, USA.
Rosemary Radford Ruether is a well-known radical feminist writing from a Christian standpoint. Aiming to connect women of the First and Third Worlds, 14 writers from around the world explore the roles of religion and feminism in the context of environmental crisis in Latin America, Asia, and Africa. They link the domination of women to the domination of nature, and show how religion has often reinforced this domination. Calls for a creative synthesis of what women find to be liberating in their religious or spiritual heritage.

Feminist Theology From the Third World: A Reader, Ursula King (ed.), 1994, 1996, Society for Promoting Christian Knowledge (SPCK), Orbis Books.

A collection of 38 essays looking at theology from a Third-World perspective, using sources from Africa, Asia, and Latin America, as well as Israel and the Pacific region.

With Passion and Compassion: Third World Women Doing Theology: Reflections from the Women's Commission of the Ecumenical Association of Third World Theologians, Virginia Fabella and M. Amba Oduyoye, 1988, Orbis Books.

A collection of writings by women from the Third World who each consider what it means to be a Christian and a woman in the Third World. United in their attempts to create their own liberative theology, this book looks at the different problems faced in different regions.

Sexism and God-Talk: Towards a Feminist Theology, Rosemary Radford Ruether, 1983, 1986, SCM Press Ltd, London.

This classic book, focusing on Christianity, uses feminist insights to expose the socially constructed roots of classical theology. It also points to a link between the exploitation of women, and human destruction of the Earth.

Women Before God, Lavinia Byrne, 1988, 1995, SPCK.

Reflects on both the past and the future of the Christian Church, and on a Catholic woman's relationship to the agenda of Christian feminism.

Women Divided: Gender, Religion and Politics in Northern Ireland, Rosemary Sales, 1997. Routledge, 11 New Fetter Lane, London EC4P 4EE, UK.

This book focuses on the relationship between gender and sectarian divisions between Roman Catholics and Protestants in Northern Ireland. It looks at the impact of the conflict on women, and the ways in which they have developed their own agendas for change, while largely excluded from formal politics.

Overcoming Violence: The Challenge to the Church in All Places, Margot Kassmann, Risk Book Series, World Council of Churches Publications. PO Box 2100, 150 Rue de Ferney, 1211 Geneva 2, Switzerland.

In a world of so much violence, this short book asks whether the churches can live out their conviction that war is against God's will. It examines Christian resources for non-violent resolution of conflict, and considers the opportunities and problems faced by people committed to non-violence. Includes a chapter on how women and children are affected by violence.

Women of Fire and Spirit: History, Faith and Gender in Roho Region in Western Kenya, Cynthia Hoehler-Fatton, 1996. Oxford University Press, Walton Street, Oxford, OX2 6DP, UK.

A book tracing the role of women in the evolution and expansion of the Roho ('Holy Spirit') churches of western Kenya. It uses women's oral histories to challenge previous histories of the Roho Church, and goes on to examine how women's roles within the Church have declined in recent decades.

Valuing Spirituality in Development: Initial considerations regarding the creation of spiritually-based indicators for development, Baha'i Publishing Trust, 27 Rutland Gate, London SW7 1PD, UK.

Baha'i communities operate more than 1,300 local development projects throughout the world. Believers assert that what sets Baha'i apart from other world religions is its integration of spiritual, social, and administrative principles. This concept paper was written for the World Faiths and Development Dialogue, Lambeth Palace, London, 18-19 February 1998. It gives the Baha'i perspective on human development and discusses the need for spiritually-based indicators of development. Equality between the sexes is seen as one of the five foundational principles of human development, as is 'unity in diversity'; but the document remains at a visionary level without indicating how such a vision could be brought about.

Feminist Theology, Sheffield University Press, Mansion House, 19 Kingfield Road, Sheffield, S11 9AS. Phone: +44 (114) 255 4433; fax: +44 (114) 255 4626.
An academic journal covering all areas of theology.

Womanspirit, 52 Rosemount Court, Booterstown, Co. Dublin, Eire.
Includes news, articles, book reviews, poems, and letters from believers of Christian and Jewish backgrounds throughout the world. Central themes include raising awareness of the oppression of women and working towards inclusive religious attitudes.

Women in Judaism, Dept of Near and Middle Eastern Civilizations, University of Toronto, 4 Bancroft Avenue, Toronto, ON, Canada M5S 1C1
http:// www.utoronto.ca/wjudaism/journal
A new journal published exclusively on the internet offering scholarly debate on gender related issues in Judaism. Examines both ancient and modern issues on Jewish religion, culture, and society.

Video

Battle for the minds, Produced and directed by Steven Lipscomb, New Day Films, Dept WM, 22-D Hollywood Avenue, Hohokus, New Jersey 07423, US.
Phone: +1 (800) 343 5540 (ordering information); e-mail: tmcndy@aol.com
http:// www.battleforthemnds.com
Documents the fundamentalist takeover within the US Southern Baptist Convention, which has 40,000 churches in the US and nearly 15,000,000 members. This film reveals the careful political manipulation behind the takeover, as well as the repercussions within the denomination. At the core of the film is the question of women's proper role within the seminary and the denomination, told in women's own words.

Organisations

Women Living Under Muslim Laws, BP 23, 34790 Grabels, Montpellier, France.
Phone: +33 (467) 109 166, fax: +33 (467) 109 167. E-mail: wluml@mnet.fr
An international organisation which 'addresses itself to women living where Islam is the religion of the state; as well as to women who belong to Muslim communities ruled by minority religious laws; to women in secular states where Islam is rapidly expanding, and where fundamentalists demand a minority religious law; as well as to women from immigrant Muslim communities in Europe and the Americas; and to non-Muslim women, either nationals or foreigners, living in Muslim countries and communities, where Muslim laws are applied to them and to their children'. Formed in 1984, WLUML has campaigned internationally for women's human rights. It aims to create links between women and women's groups, increase women's knowledge about their what their rights are, and how to assert these in their particular contexts.

Women Against Fundamentalism, BM Box 2706, London WC1 3XX, UK.
A feminist network, campaigning against fundamentalism in all religions, and for sexual and political freedom all over the world. Launched in 1989, it believes that fundamentalism is basically political, and that the control of women is central to fundamentalism in all religions. Publishes a journal, *Women Against Fundamentalism,* which looks at a range of international issues.

Sakyadita: International Association of Women in Buddhism, 16 Nun Street, Lancaster, LA1 3JP, UK. Phone: 01524 844 719; fax: 0181 802 0628;
e-mail: kawanami@lancaster.as.uk
An international group of women active in Buddhism, which produces a newsletter and organises conferences every two years, usually held in developing countries.

Conspirando, Casilla 371-11, Correo Nunoa, Santiago, Chile.
A network of Latin American women committed to eco-feminism, theology and spirituality.

Sisterhood is Global Institute
4343 Montgomery Avenue, Suite 201, Bethesda, MD 20814, USA. Phone: +1 (301) 657 4355; fax: +1 (301) 657 4381; e-mail: sigi@igc.apc.org. http://www.sigi.org
A non-profit organisation promoting women's rights through human-rights education projects. Their work focuses on women living in Islamic countries, and includes advocacy programmes, appeals against human-rights abuses, and participation in international conferences. Their internet site includes a newsletter, a publications page, and information on their human-rights work.

World Council of Muslim Women Foundation
http://www.connect.ab.ca/~Ifahlman/wcomwf.htm
A non-profit organisation 'dedicated as a living memoral to the women of Bosnia, and other women who have suffered the degradation of rape, torture and death. Focuses on education for women's rights, global peace and interfaith education from a worldwide perspective'.

The World Council of Churches, PO Box 2100, 1211 Geneva 2, Switzerland.
Phone: +41 (22) 791 6111; fax: +41 (22) 791 0361; e-mail: info@wcc-coe.org
http://www.wcc.coe.org/
A fellowship of churches from nearly all the Christian traditions, representing over 122 countries in all continents. Works towards justice and continuing renewal of the Christian faith. Their web site can be read in English, French, German, or Spanish, and offers information on WCC's work, history, publications, and events. Has a Women's Unit.

Interchurch Organisation for Development Cooperation, PO Box 151, 3700 AD Zeist, The Netherlands. E-mail: admin@icco.nl
Write for news of campaigns, and details of publications.

CAFOD (Catholic Fund for Overseas Development), 2 Romero Close, Stockwell Road, London SW9 9TY, UK. Phone: +44 (171) 733 7900.
Committed to addressing gender issues in its development and relief work in developing countries across the world.

Christian Aid, PO Box 100, London SE1 7RT, UK. Phone: +44 (171) 620 4444; fax: +44 (171) 620 0719
Christian Aid works throughout the world in partnership with communities of all faiths in developing countries, and campaigns on issues of justice and poverty.

Catholic Institute for International Relations, Unit 3, Canonbury Yard, 190a New North Road, London N1 7BJ, UK.
CIIR is part of the UK government's volunteer programme for developing countries, offering technical assistance and support.

Women in Theology, 19a Compton Terrace, London N1 2UN, UK. Phone: +44 (171) 354 3631.
Aims to empower women in a spiritual context. Promotes inclusive language and works to create opportunities for feminist theology. Looks at new forms of worship and ministry, and also runs local groups.

Web resources

http://www.women3rdworld.tqn.com/msub8.htm
A site about women in the Third World which links users to a range of other sites relating to Christianity, Islam, Judaism, and Hinduism. Also includes news, articles, letters, and a noticeboard.

Islam and Women's Rights
http://www.arches.uga.edu/~godlas/Islamwomen.html

FEMREL-L
Established as a forum for open and stimulating discussion about women, religion, and feminist theology. Subscribe by e-mailing LISTSERV@listserv.aol.com with the message SUBSCRIBE FEMREL-L followed by your own name.

Bridges
Describes itself as a 'moderated list' which explores Jewish feminist identity and considers Jewish and female existence and activism in relation to movements for change. Subscribe by e-mailing: listserv@israel.nysernet.org

Conspirando (see organisations)
http://www.teologica feminista latinamericana
A Spanish language web page.

Women Active in Buddhism
http://members.tripod.com/~Lhamo
An on-line magazine with details of teachers, resources, books, and organisations of relevance for women following the Buddhist tradition. Accessible and fun, with lots of useful information.

inclusivechurch
http://www.inclusivechurch.org/
An American web site open to anyone who wants to discuss topics related to women in the Catholic Church. Visitors can post ideas for debate or reply to previous messages.